D0560141

HONEST ABE

HONEST ABE

101 LITTLE-KNOWN TRUTHS

ABOUT ABRAHAM LINCOLN

Brian Thornton *Foreword by* Richard W. Donley

Aadamsmedia

Avon, Massachusetts

For my grandmothers, Jean Thornton and Dorothy Inman.
One was born on Lincoln's birthday.
The other called him the only Republican for whom she would have ever voted.

———————

Published by
Adams Media, a division of F+W Media, Inc.
57 Littlefield Street, Avon, MA 02322. U.S.A.
www.adamsmedia.com

Previously published as *101 Things You Didn't Know about Lincoln* by Brian Thornton,
copyright © 2006 by F+W Media, Inc., ISBN 10: 1-59337-399-6, ISBN 13: 978-1-59337-399-3.

ISBN 10: 1-4405-1230-2
ISBN 13: 978-1-4405-1230-8
eISBN 10: 1-4405-1231-0
eISBN 13: 978-1-4405-1231-5

Printed in the United States of America.

10 9 8 7 6 5 4 3 2 1

Library of Congress Cataloging-in-Publication Data
is available from the publisher.

This book is available at quantity discounts for bulk purchases.
For information, please call 1-800-289-0963.

Acknowledgments

Someone who knew the young Abraham Lincoln well once said of Abe that he was so poor that he had nothing but friends. Someone else, whose name I don't recall, once said that a man with friends is rich beyond imagining. I agree with that, and this being my first book, I'm beholden to an awful lot of people. I'd like to take a moment to thank them.

First, I'd like to thank Richard W. Donley for being a first-rate graduate school mentor and friend, to say nothing of writing the foreword for this book. Then there are other scholars who helped along the way, like Martin Seedorf from Eastern Washington University, and Robert Carricker, Stephen Balzarini, and the late Tim Sarbaugh at Gonzaga. Thanks to all of you for contributing to a first-rate education.

Also, thanks to my family and friends: my parents, Hal and Berniece, and my brother Paul, for believing in the writer as well as in the project. Seattle-area writer and friend David Morel gave wonderful feedback and generously looked over my work, helping with the seemingly endless polishing process. My attorney friend Cynthia Patterson contributed mightily to the research I did on Lincoln's approach to the law, and is solely responsible for putting me on the trail of Lincoln's "chicken bone case."

Then of course, there's the team at Adams Media. Director of Product Development Paula Munier believed that I had a book on Lincoln in me, and offered me the opportunity to get that book out of my system and onto the book racks. My project editor and designated task-mistress, Andrea Mattei, worked tirelessly on shaping my output into something coherent and readable. If you liked the pace, enjoyed the narrative flow, and found elements of this book interesting, thank her. Goodness knows that *I* can't thank her enough for all of her hard work. You're a workhorse, Andrea, and I'm grateful for the opportunity to pull in the traces with such a consummate professional.

January 7, 2011
Seattle, WA

Contents

Part 2
The Middle Years: Lincoln in Springfield / 53

Part 3
Lincoln and the U.S. Presidency / 125

Part 4
Lincoln and the Civil War / 149

Part 5
Comparisons and Contemporaries / 203

Part 6
Lincoln and His Legacy / 225

Works Consulted / 233
Index / 235

Foreword

Senator Everett Dirksen of Illinois once noted that politicians of all persuasions had to "get right" with Lincoln. While this statement no doubt was, in part, made in jest, it does in a small way indicate the pervasiveness of Lincoln's influence on American history since his death in 1865. It's safe to say that more has been written about Abraham Lincoln than any other American.

Every aspect of Lincoln's life has been explored and analyzed by dozens upon dozens of noted historians over the past century, as well as a legion of writers of questionable skill and purpose. Lincoln's speeches and writings have been a source of inspiration for many over the past century and a half. Sometimes, by either distortion or misquoting, he has even been enlisted in causes he would have shunned had he a choice.

Possibly the most disturbing aspect of the Lincoln story is the shroud of myth that has enveloped him over the decades, and has, in a sense, hidden this extraordinary leader and politician from the general population. Almost all of us were brought up on stories of Lincoln the humble lad reading by firelight, his legendary honesty, his feats as a rail-splitter, and hundreds of other tales about his life, be they true or not. Every nation needs its mythic heroes, but in the case of Lincoln, the facts alone make a fascinating story.

As Brian Thornton notes in his introduction, it is his purpose to go behind the iconic figure that Lincoln has become for many, and present to the general reader of history a more human Lincoln to whom we can all relate. Mr. Thornton has not taken the standard biographical approach to Lincoln. Instead, he has looked at various parts of the Lincoln story, some oft-told and some not so well known, to bring us a Lincoln who is a man of incredible accomplishments and a man who is at the same time quite flawed. In other words, he presents the reader with an Abraham Lincoln who is very much like all of us, and at the same time unlike any other American before or since.

—*Richard W. Donley, professor emeritus of nineteenth-century American history at Eastern Washington University Cheney, WA January 2011*

Introduction

There are few historical figures as beloved as Abraham Lincoln. The national monument erected in his honor dominates an entire end of the Mall in our nation's capital. He is one of the most recognizable icons our society has ever produced.

Unfortunately, an "icon" in the truest sense of the word is a religious image, either a painting or a statue. Americans tend to revere the icon that history has made of Abraham Lincoln without really understanding the flesh-and-blood man behind it.

This is a shame, because the man himself is fascinating enough without all of the trappings of myth that have sprung up in the 140 years since his death. Abraham Lincoln was a man. He was good and he was bad, and like many good American heroes, he was keenly aware of his faults. The resulting humility that others found so endearing both during his lifetime and in the years since his untimely death is a distinctly American character trait. We love for our heroes to be modest.

And yet Abraham Lincoln was so much more than that grave-faced image sitting on the throne in Washington, D.C. A skilled, charming politician, a genius at reading people, a devoted family man, Lincoln was literally the right man at the right time to step forward in his country's darkest hour and be that rarest of men: a leader. He was also a religious skeptic, a frequently inattentive husband, terribly shy around single women, given to bouts of deep depression, and possessed of a short memory when it came to personal friendships. These perceived shortcomings should not be swept into the dustbin of history. Rather, they lend color, perspective, and shading to the polished white marble of one of our favorite statues, showing a man all the more remarkable for possessing these faults.

If you're going to understand this extraordinary man, it is important to humanize the legend, to show him and his extraordinary accomplishments in context. Abraham Lincoln was a remarkable human being who transcended his humble origins, overcame early tragedy, and ascended to the highest office in the land. But that is only half of the story. The intent of this book is to educate as well as entertain, to give Lincoln the man back to the people who so love him. After all, they have more reason to do so than they know.

Part 1

Personal Background and Early Life

Sure, we know that Abraham Lincoln was president—
after all, he's on the penny and the five-dollar bill.
But what was his childhood like? What
was his family life like? What was his
world like before he achieved fame first
as a state legislator, then as a great trial
lawyer, and finally as president?
Read on to find out. . . .

1 What was Lincoln's middle name?

The mystery of Abraham Lincoln's middle name can be answered by looking to one of his ancestors, who was named, of all things, Abraham Lincoln. Our sixteenth president was named after his paternal grandfather, a successful Virginia farmer who sold the 210-acre Rockingham County farm his own father had left him, and relocated his entire family to Kentucky in the mid-1780s. Abraham Lincoln the elder was killed in 1786 during an Indian attack while planting a cornfield on the Jefferson County homestead he'd established there.

Although the two Abrahams never knew each other, they did have one thing in common: Neither of them had a middle name. This was not unusual on the frontier in the late eighteenth and early nineteenth centuries. Thomas Lincoln, son of one and father to the other of these two Abrahams, had no middle name either.

Abraham Lincoln the younger broke this tradition with three of his four sons, giving them each middle names. Abraham named his eldest Robert Todd, giving the child his mother's maiden name as his middle name (another time-honored tradition). His second son (who died of tuberculosis just short of his fourth birthday) was named Edward Baker, after a lifelong friend. William Wallace, his third son, was named after his uncle, the physician husband of Mary Todd Lincoln's sister Frances. Lincoln named his last son after his own father, right down to forgoing a middle name for the boy.

2 The truth about Lincoln's parents and siblings

Abraham Lincoln, roundly lauded as the greatest president in American history, is all the more beloved because he came from "common stock." Americans love rooting for the underdog, and Abraham Lincoln began life as exactly that. Born in a log cabin and raised on the frontier by illiterate parents, he overcame the handicaps of his birth and his upbringing through hard work.

Despite their illiteracy, Lincoln's parents were hardly unaccomplished ne'er-do-wells. His father, Thomas Lincoln, was a talented carpenter and a successful farmer. His mother, Nancy Hanks Lincoln, was a skilled seamstress. In Lincoln's day, illiteracy was far more common in America than it is today. Lincoln himself had less than a year of formal education.

Born the third son of a wealthy Virginia farmer in 1778, Thomas moved with his family to Kentucky while still very young. Thomas's father sold his large and prosperous farm in the mid-1780s, planning to establish an even larger one in Kentucky. But his father's unexpected death in 1786 left Thomas dispossessed and penniless because, according to property law at that time, when a man died, his eldest son inherited his entire estate. As a result, Thomas Lincoln went from being the son of a well-to-do plantation owner to being a destitute orphan. He grew up working as a farm laborer and carpenter, until he met Nancy Hanks in 1806.

The most interesting thing about Lincoln's parentage is that he was so obviously embarrassed by his parents once he became a successful attorney (by this time his mother had died). He and his father didn't understand each other or communicate well, and although fond of his stepmother, Sarah, Lincoln never introduced either of them to his wife. In fact, he didn't even invite them to his wedding, and neither of them ever met any of his children.

And what about siblings? Did Lincoln have any brothers and sisters? Actually, he had one of each. His younger brother, Thomas, was born sometime after 1811 and died in infancy. Little is known about him. His sister, Sarah, was two years his senior, and died in childbirth in 1828.

 ## The proximity of Lincoln's and Jefferson Davis's birthplaces

Many people know that Abraham Lincoln was born during a thunderstorm early on Sunday morning, February 12, 1809. Most people don't realize that his birthplace at Hodgkins Creek, in Hardin County, Kentucky, was less than 100 miles from the spot in neighboring Christian (now Todd) County where his future adversary, Jefferson Davis, was born less than eight months previously.

These two men, both Kentuckians by birth and born less than a year apart, had little else in common. Davis's wealthy family moved to a plantation in northern Mississippi while he was still an infant. Lincoln's impoverished family tried to make a go of it in Kentucky for several years, and when they did move, they moved north, across the Ohio, and settled in Indiana. They moved that direction at least in part because Lincoln's father, Thomas, opposed the practice of slavery.

Funny how two men who had such an impact on the course of American history came from virtually the same region of the same state, were born within a year of each other, and then took disparate paths to a great confrontation in their later years. It is also worth noting that, like Hodgkins Creek and Christian County, Washington, D.C., and Richmond, Virginia (the Confederate capital), are less than 100 miles apart.

4   Was Lincoln really born in a log cabin?

Much has been made of Abraham Lincoln's rise from poverty, including his birth in a log cabin in Kentucky in 1809. But was he really born in a log cabin? Many American presidents have pointed to their birth in a log cabin as proof of their humble origins. Historically, this sort of political posturing has played well with voters, making the case that said politician, despite looking and dressing and acting like a member of the upper classes, really was "one of the common people." For instance, Andrew Jackson played up his modest upbringing and tapped into a new group of voters: frontier farmers. This led to the politics of the "common man," afterward dubbed "Jacksonian Democracy" in American politics.

William Henry Harrison was truly the first "log cabin" candidate, born in a log cabin in Virginia. However, Harrison was not the son of a frontier farmer. He was the scion of a fine Virginia family born in the log cabin *around which his father's new plantation house was built*. In other words, Harrison was a ringer.

For the next forty or so years, this was the case with nearly every presidential candidate who claimed to be a plainspoken, sober, hard-working man of the people. Most of them were simply rich men with some sort of frontier connection they worked to maximum political advantage. With one notable exception, none of them came from poor frontier families. Only Abraham Lincoln could truly make that claim.

Just as the legend says, Abraham Lincoln *really was* born in a log cabin to a poor pioneer family. Some sources have maintained that he was actually born in what was called a "half-face camp," a sort of lean-to with one open side, common on the Kentucky frontier. Particulars aside, you get the point.

Lincoln was very young when the family moved from his birthplace, so he had no personal recollection of it. However, a neighbor once called it "a barren waste." Unlike the original homes of those other future presidents, these were hardly the grounds upon which Virginia plantations were later built.

Lincoln actually did transcend humble origins, and as such, oddly enough, he turned out to be the exception that proved the rule. It is no accident that subsequent presidential candidates tried to work the log cabin angle. From 1868 onward, though, they did it more to show how they "were just like Lincoln," not Jackson.

It's ironic when you think about it. Abraham Lincoln hated farm work, and so he got away from the fields and frontier life just as fast as he could. He never shot an Indian. He never fought a duel. By the time he won election to the presidency, he was a former U.S. congressman and arguably one of the most successful trial lawyers in the country. Yet to this day he is remembered as "Honest Abe, the rail-splitter. Born in a log cabin, you know!"

5 Was Lincoln's mother illegitimate?

No one knows for sure. Nancy Hanks was born in Hampshire County, in what is now West Virginia, on February 5, 1784. Her mother's name was Lucy Hanks, but beyond that, no one knows much about Nancy's relationship with her birth mother, except that they weren't particularly close. Even less is known about Nancy's father, although Abraham Lincoln did once remark to his law partner, William H. Herndon, that his maternal grandfather was "a well-bred Virginia farmer or planter."

Soon after Nancy's mother married—perhaps for the first time—Nancy went to live with her aunt and uncle, Elizabeth and Thomas Sparrow. In those days, children of unmarried mothers were often shipped off to other relatives. Many folks on the frontier believed that children born out of wedlock carried the mark of the "sin" that created them. And, so, they were often an embarrassment to their "upright" parents later in life—kind of like a living reminder of earlier "sins." This was probably the case with Nancy Hanks Lincoln.

Given this situation, it's no surprise that Elizabeth was actually more of a mother to Nancy than Lucy was. In fact, Nancy was so close to her aunt Elizabeth and uncle Thomas, she began using the name Nancy Sparrow.

In spite of the disadvantages of her birth situation, Nancy was a woman of strong character. Abraham Lincoln certainly spoke highly of his mother: "God bless my mother; all that I am or ever hope to be I owe to her."

True to her son's remarks, nearly all sources agree that Nancy Hanks Lincoln was intelligent, kind, and religious. She was able to read, but she could only write enough to sign her name. A hard worker, Nancy was a talented seamstress—a skill she learned from her aunt Elizabeth. Although these details demonstrate what kind of person Nancy was, no one knows for sure what she actually looked like. She died well before the age of photography, and no one ever drew her picture. If you're hoping to form an image of Lincoln's mother in your mind, you can't even rely on other people's reports—contemporaries described her as everything from tall and lean to short and stout!

6   How Lincoln repeatedly escaped death as a child

It's a well-known maxim of American history that life on the advancing frontier was difficult, far more so than "modern" readers can conceive. Lincoln's life was no exception to this rule. In addition to poor diet, conflict with understandably hostile Native American tribes, wild animals, extremely cold weather, and the arduous task of clearing forest and planting fields, the specter of disease loomed large, and only the most primitive health care was available. Twice in 1818 alone, Abraham Lincoln cheated death: first, when kicked in the head by a horse; second, when a frontier malady wiped out almost half of the family he had in the area.

One of young Abraham's chores when he was growing up was taking a load of corn by horse to a gristmill some two miles away from the family farm. He would then hitch the horse to the mill and lead it around in circles, thereby grinding the corn into meal.

One particular day, Lincoln had to wait for a long time while those who had arrived at the mill before him ground their corn. Since he got off to a late start that day, he was worried about finishing up and making it home while there was still daylight. And so he took his impatience out on the old mare he was using to grind the meal. As the afternoon shadows lengthened, Lincoln lashed the poor animal after her every turn working the corn mill, trying to get her to go faster.

Finally, the mare had enough. She raised her hindquarters and kicked the boy square in the middle of his forehead, bloodying him and knocking him unconscious to the ground. The mill owner, a man named Noah Gordon, came running. At first he thought the boy was dead, and immediately sent for his father.

Thomas Lincoln took his son home and put him to bed, where he laid unconscious overnight. After awakening, Abraham was unable to speak for several hours, but he eventually made a full recovery. He suffered no apparent long-term physical or neurological damage, although it's possible that his occasional deep bouts of depression might have arisen in part from this accident.

Later that same year, an epidemic of "milk sickness" struck the community of Little Pigeon Creek, Indiana, where the Lincolns then made their home. Homesteaders in the region knew that milk sickness had something to do with the milk they got from their cows (hence the name), but they were at a loss as to how it worked and what they should do to prevent it. (Not until much later was the cause of milk sickness traced to the poisonous white snakeroot plant.)

Milk sickness hit the Lincoln household particularly hard. First, it afflicted Lincoln's great-aunt and -uncle on his mother's side, Thomas and Elizabeth Sparrow. The Sparrows had come from Kentucky to Indiana to live with their niece's family after being dispossessed on account of an eviction proceeding the previous year. They both quickly succumbed to the effects of the poison.

Not long after, Nancy Lincoln, Abraham's mother, fell ill with the same malady. She lasted a week. Before she died on October 5, she said goodbye to her children from her sickbed, exhorting them to treat their father, themselves, and the world kindly. Abraham Lincoln was nine years old.

Then there's another story about how Lincoln almost drowned when he was seven. It's difficult to confirm, because it relies solely on the story told late in life by one Austin Gollaher.

Gollaher was a childhood friend and playmate of Lincoln's when the Lincoln family lived in the Knob Creek region of western Kentucky. According to Gollaher's story, the two boys were crossing a log that straddled the creek one sunny Sunday morning in 1816, when young Abraham became frightened, began to tremble, and fell into the water.

Gollaher said he grabbed a stick, used it to fish Lincoln out of the creek before he drowned, then set about reviving him, making sure to get all the water out of his lungs.

Is this the truth? It's difficult to say. After all, we only have Gollaher's word to go on. Otherwise, there's no evidence that it ever happened. If Lincoln ever told this story, it's never been recorded. Gollaher allowed for this lack of outside evidence by saying: "We promised each other that we would never tell anybody about it, and never did for years. I never told any one of it until after Lincoln was killed." One thing's for certain: Only Lincoln and Gollaher, who waited until shortly before his death in 1898 to record this story, knew for sure. And neither one of them is talking.

 ## 7 Was Lincoln's family really poor?

To answer this question, you need to consider ideas about frontier land owner- ship and poverty in Lincoln's day. It is an established part of the Lincoln myth that he grew up in extreme poverty. Lincoln himself once referred to the story of his upbringing as "the annals of the poor." True enough, Lincoln's family was cash poor, but they weren't exactly poverty-stricken.

Income levels mean nothing in a vacuum. In a market economy, what mat- ters is purchasing power. It means little to say that Lincoln's family was poor, because they lived in a barter economy. In other words, when Lincoln was growing up, all of his neighbors were cash-poor farmers, too.

Now, being cash poor is different from being flat-out poor. Except for the family's second Kentucky farm on Knob Creek, Abraham's father, Thomas, always owned the land he worked. (In the case of Knob Creek, Thomas thought he had paid for a certain section of land when he bought his farm, but competing land claims encroached on that.) Knowing that he didn't have the money to win a legal battle over who owned what, Thomas abandoned his Kentucky claim.

He moved his family across the Ohio River, into southwestern Indiana, where he bought and cleared land along Little Pigeon Creek. Being cash poor, he paid for the Indiana claim in installments, but when he moved to Illinois years later, he sold the property in Indiana for cash, which he then used to buy his new farm.

So it's fair to say that Lincoln's boyhood tore a page from "the annals of the poor," as long as you realize that he didn't grow up a beggar in the streets, and he rarely went hungry. Being this sort of poor was just part and parcel of life on the American frontier.

8 Lincoln's real relationship with his father

We tend to think of Abraham Lincoln as a great president, a capable leader, and an honorable and admirable man. Part of the problem with carving marble statues of the great men in our history is that we frequently lose sight of their humanity. There's a lot more to these people than what they did to make them famous.

Abraham Lincoln was a man, too. And he struggled with the sorts of mundane family issues that we take for granted. Like many human beings both today and throughout history, Abraham Lincoln did not get along well with one of his parents. In Lincoln's case, the trouble was with his father.

Lincoln's father, Thomas, was born in Rockingham County, Virginia, on January 6, 1778, the fourth of five children born to Abraham and Bathsheba Lincoln. Thomas Lincoln grew to be a man very different from his famous son. Whereas his son was extremely tall, especially for the time (6'4"), Thomas was just a bit above average height (5'9"). Whereas Abraham hungered to learn and read every book he could get his hands on, Thomas Lincoln was a functional illiterate, who only learned to write his own name (and poorly, at that). Although he made attempts to encourage Abraham's love of learning, the elder Lincoln never seemed to understand what good could come of his son's attempts to better himself.

Lincoln's stepmother, Sarah, recalled years later that although her husband didn't really understand the importance of an education, nor his son's thirst for knowledge, he did nothing to discourage it. According to her, "As a usual thing Mr. [Thomas] Lincoln never made Abe quit reading to do anything if he could avoid it. He would do it himself first. Mr. Lincoln could read a little and could scarcely write his own name," and like so many parents, he wanted better for his child than he himself had. Thus, he made sure that his son had opportunities "to learn and he encouraged him to do it in all ways he could."

Lincoln's cousin Dennis Hanks remembered a different side of Lincoln's father. According to Hanks, on more than one occasion Thomas Lincoln had "sometimes to slash [Abraham] for neglecting his work by reading." Abraham undoubtedly remembered Thomas as an obstacle to his education, and it helps explain his later behavior toward his father.

In his defense, Thomas Lincoln never had even the meager opportunities his own son had when it came to schooling. Only eight years old when his father was struck down during an Indian attack, young Thomas grew up fast. His elder brother, Mordecai, inherited all of their father's estate, leaving Thomas to fend for himself at a young age.

Thomas earned his living predominantly as a farm laborer and a carpenter before buying his own farm and marrying Lincoln's mother. For the rest of his life, Thomas Lincoln earned his keep either by farming his own land, doing carpentry work, or hiring out his teenaged son as a laborer.

Young Abraham resented this, and as he grew to manhood he became more and more determined to pursue an altogether different path from his father's. Although he dutifully worked every job to which his father sent him, and just as dutifully handed over all of the wages he earned to Thomas (a legal requirement until he turned twenty-one), his disdain for his father, and all that he represented, continued to grow.

Abraham and his father also disagreed profoundly on religion. Whereas Thomas Lincoln was a lifelong churchgoer, Abraham grew up suspicious of organized religion. Although conversant with the Bible and an acknowledged Christian, the younger Lincoln rarely attended services and never joined any congregation. These and other differences helped drive the wedge further between the two.

The elder Lincoln could not understand his son, and it is clear that, for all of his great intelligence and easy humor (which he supposedly inherited from his father), Abraham Lincoln understood his father no better. Once the young Lincoln turned twenty-one, he left his father's house and moved to New Salem, Illinois. He visited infrequently after that, and relations between him and his father were always strained.

Later in life, Lincoln seemed embarrassed by his poorly educated, unsophisticated father. This was never more apparent than when Lincoln married Mary Todd in November 1842. He did not invite his father.

9 Lincoln's relationship with his "angel mother" and his stepmother

As mentioned earlier in this section, Abraham Lincoln's birth mother died when he was only nine years old. Later in life, he said that although he barely recalled what she had looked like, he always remembered her kindness and caring. Without question, his mother's early death had a tremendous impact on the little boy.

When Abraham met his new stepmother, Sarah Bush Johnston, she could tell that he was starved for love. Eventually, Lincoln differentiated his relationships with the two women by calling Sarah his mother and referring to his dead birth mother, Nancy Hanks, as his "angel mother."

Sarah brought order and warmth to the Lincoln household, which had been without a woman's touch for many months. She made a point of treating Abraham and his sister, Sarah, as if they were her own (she had three children from her first marriage), and they responded strongly to that. She was particularly fond of Abraham, calling him, "the best boy I ever saw."

Sarah encouraged her stepson in his studies, allowing him to read from her family Bible (like Abraham's birth mother, she was illiterate) and her copy of *Robinson Crusoe*. She also stuck up for Abraham when his father grumbled that his studies took time away from the plowing and the planting.

Abraham repaid Sarah's kindness by looking out for her after his father died in 1851. Several years earlier, he had already purchased part of his father's farm to help Thomas meet his debts. Once Thomas died, Abraham bought forty acres and set them aside, "for Mother while she lives."

On the other hand, he never introduced Sarah to his wife and family, even after his father died. (Many people believed that Thomas was the reason Abraham didn't invite his parents to his wedding.) It is possible that he was embarrassed by his stepmother's illiteracy, or by the humble cabin in which she lived out her days. After all, Mary Todd had grown up on a plantation, and she was not above putting on airs.

Shortly after he was elected president, Lincoln made a last trip down to see his stepmother in her cabin on Goosenest Prairie, and they visited his father's grave. That time, their parting was particularly sad, because Sarah had a premonition that Lincoln was going to his doom. She told Lincoln's law partner, William H. Herndon, about it later: "I did not want Abe to run for president—did not want him elected—was afraid somehow or other—felt it in my heart that something would happen [to] him and when he came down to see me that something would befall Abe and that I should see him no more."

She was right. Abraham Lincoln died at the hands of an assassin in 1865, without ever returning home to Illinois. When Herndon visited Sarah shortly before her death in 1870, she told him, "Abe and his father are in Heaven I have no doubt, and I want to go there—go where they are. God bless Abraham."

10 "The wedding-bed prank"

In 1828, approximately eighteen months after her marriage to a neighbor named Aaron Grigsby, Abraham Lincoln's older sister, Sarah Lincoln Grigsby, died in childbirth outside of Gentryville, Indiana. News of her death understandably devastated her younger brother. He felt the Grigsby family had been negligent in caring for his ailing sister, and he resented them for it. He also publicly questioned why the Grigsbys didn't call in a doctor to tend to Sarah sooner. Within a year of his sister's death, Lincoln's feud with the Grigsbys led him to play the most impressive practical joke in a lifetime full of them: the so-called wedding-bed prank.

In 1829, two of Aaron Grigsby's male relatives got married in a spring double wedding. Lincoln was not invited. Reportedly, Lincoln was insulted when Reuben Grigsby Jr. and Charles Grigsby did not include any of the Lincoln clan on their nuptial guest list. In retaliation, Lincoln contrived to have each of the bridegrooms escorted to the wrong wedding bed after the wedding reception. The deception was immediately (and hilariously) discovered, but tongues started wagging afterward regardless.

Lincoln did his best to keep the gossip flowing around town. To satirize the event, he composed a terrible poem called "The Chronicles of Reuben." Although the poem was supposed to read like a Bible verse, it sounded more like a dirty limerick. After he recounted the tale of the misplaced bridegrooms, he wrote more stanzas describing the fictitious jilting of another Grigsby brother:

You cursed baldhead,

My suitor you never can be;

Besides, your low crotch proclaims you a botch

And that never can answer for me.

This bit of "epic" writing was so popular that, years later, one pioneer from the area claimed folks still remembered some pieces of it "better than the Bible." Unfortunately, Lincoln's thoughts on the timelessness of his verse, and the prank that inspired it, are not recorded.

11 The question of Lincoln's education

In terms of his childhood education, Lincoln's experience was pretty typical of people growing up on the frontier. As such, his level of articulation and his superb ability to write so many great speeches are our most lasting testaments to his genius. This ability to captivate the imaginations of those around him seems all the more amazing when you realize that Abraham Lincoln had less than a year of formal schooling. He was almost completely a self-taught man.

Lincoln demonstrated a voracious appetite for learning. He attributed this lifelong hunger for knowledge to his mother, Nancy. His illiterate stepmother, Sarah, did her best to encourage the boy as well. She brought several books of her own into the household when she married Lincoln's father, including a family Bible. She recalled that her famous stepson read it occasionally, though not as much as is sometimes said.

Sarah also had other books, including John Bunyan's *Pilgrim's Progress* and Aesop's fables. Bunyan's book influenced the cadences of Lincoln's later political speeches. Aesop's fables had such an impact on him that he memorized entire stories and could write them out if needed. This book, too, with its morals provided at the end of each tale, affected Lincoln throughout his life. The famous "house divided" speech Lincoln gave, upon being nominated as the Republican candidate for a U.S. Senate seat from Illinois, reflected the moral of Aesop's story of "The Lion and the Four Bulls": "A kingdom divided against itself cannot stand."

Lincoln read as much history as he could lay his hands on. What little time he spent in public school gave him a solid grounding in mathematics. Shortly after his mother died and his father remarried, Lincoln attended the subscription school of a justice of the peace named Andrew Crawford. He only went for a single term, but he took a lot away from the experience. His cousin John Hanks noted this, later saying that Lincoln was "somewhat dull . . . not a brilliant boy, but *worked* his way by toil: to learn was hard for him, but he worked slowly, but surely."

In dismissing Lincoln as an unintelligent plodder John Hanks missed an aspect of Lincoln's personality that his stepmother, Sarah Bush Johnston Lincoln, did not. "He must understand every thing—even the smallest thing—minutely and exactly," she said. Lincoln "would then repeat it over and over to himself again and again—some times in one form and then in an other and when it was fixed in his mind to suit him he . . . never lost that fact or his understanding of it."

This was a young man who would read a book as he walked from place to place, carried one with him when he plowed fields, stopping at the end of every furrow to read a page or two. This was a mind hungry for ideas, chafing at the backwardness and lack of education he saw around him.

"Abe the Rail-Splitter": Was he really a hard-working farmhand?

In May of 1860 the Illinois Republican Party met at Decatur, Illinois, in a massive structure called a wigwam (after the Indian dwelling of the same name), constructed especially for their annual state convention. The most pressing business before the convention was that of choosing a nominee for governor.

Almost as an afterthought, the Illinois Republican Party gave favorite local son Abraham Lincoln a token endorsement for the nomination in the coming presidential race. Lincoln's endorsement was viewed as merely a courtesy because he stood little chance against contenders such as Senator William Seward of New York and Governor Salmon P. Chase of Ohio.

However, some of Lincoln's most ardent supporters had other ideas, and set about finding for Lincoln an image that would serve him as well as "Log Cabin and Hard Cider" had served Whig presidential candidate William Henry Harrison in 1840. One of these men, a politically savvy Decatur native named

Richard Oglesby, talked to several of Lincoln's closest friends and relatives, including John Hanks, a cousin on Lincoln's mother's side.

When John Hanks pointed out a rail fence that he had constructed with Lincoln's help in 1830, Oglesby had a brainstorm. With Hanks's help, he removed two of the rails and hauled them (decked out in streamers and flags) straight into the wigwam during a break in the proceedings on the first day of the convention. A label on the two rails read:

ABRAHAM LINCOLN
The Rail Candidate
FOR PRESIDENT IN 1860
Two rails from a lot of 3,000 made in 1830 by Thos. Hanks and Abe Lincoln—
whose father was the first pioneer of Macon County.

Of course the details were inaccurate. John Hanks, not Thomas Hanks, was the cousin who split those rails with Lincoln, and Lincoln's father was not the first pioneer of Macon County. However, the symbolism of this display electrified the delegates.

Lincoln stood in response to calls that he step forward and be recognized, and modestly told those assembled that he could not vouch for either of these rails being ones he had split, but that "he had mauled many and many better ones since he had grown to manhood." Immediately dubbed "the Rail-Splitter," Lincoln won the backing of his state party in his bid for the presidency in 1860. It was a crucial initial step toward the White House.

His supporters set to work marketing Lincoln as an example of the virtues of being "free soil" (anti–slave labor and pro–free labor), because of his past as a laborer. Lincoln's new image as a self-made man (which he was) went well with his folksy, storytelling, outgoing demeanor. Together, they captivated an electorate.

But just how much truth was there to the image of "Honest Abe," the humble rail-splitter? The assumption Lincoln's handlers were shooting for was that Lincoln was still close to his roots. They hoped this careful packaging would result in Lincoln's gaining votes nationwide with the same "common men" who had previously voted for Andrew "Old Hickory" Jackson and William Henry "Tippecanoe" Harrison.

The truth was that Lincoln hated country life and loathed farm labor. He considered it backbreaking and monotonous. Blessed with a keen mind and a hunger for knowledge, Lincoln made the most of his opportunities.

Until Lincoln turned twenty-one, the law at the time dictated that his father could hire him out as a farm laborer, pocketing any money he made. Once he turned twenty-one, Lincoln left his father's farm for good.

The only times Lincoln resorted to hiring himself out as a day laborer after that were when he was close to starving. Well into the late 1830s, Lincoln could be found keeping body and soul together by doing day labor, including splitting rails for fences. Once he was established as an attorney and no longer needed the extra income, Lincoln left off splitting rails, no doubt without realizing how the work he so hated would one day help him win election as president of the United States.

13 The move to New Salem, Illinois

Abraham Lincoln discovered the town of New Salem, Illinois, by accident. In 1831, he, his cousin John Hanks, and another friend ferried a flatboat they had built for storeowner and entrepreneur Denton Offutt down the Sangamon River and ran it aground on New Salem's milldam. They had a load with barrels of wheat, bacon, and corn bound for New Orleans. It took the three of them most of a day to unload the boat, and they were only able to free her from the dam because of Lincoln's ingenuity.

Offutt was so pleased by Lincoln's maneuver that he impetuously promised to open a new store in New Salem and make Lincoln its proprietor upon his return from New Orleans. For Lincoln, Offutt's offer was an opportunity to leave his father's farm and the farm labor that he hated permanently. It was also an opportunity to live in a village larger than any place he had ever lived before.

Offutt was chronically short on cash, so when his business enterprises went belly-up Lincoln was left in the lurch. He had to struggle to find work, and his income level in the raw frontier village of New Salem would be very low for the next several years, eventually requiring Lincoln to move to neighboring Springfield, where he lived until he left for Washington, D.C., in 1861.

Lincoln's career as a Mississippi River flatboatman

14

Between 1828 and 1831, Abraham Lincoln made two trips from southern Indiana to New Orleans. Each time he was a member of a crew using that flatboat to take supplies downriver for sale in New Orleans. In 1828, Lincoln accepted a job on a flatboat that a neighboring storeowner, James Gentry, was sending downriver.

At a wage of $8 per month, Lincoln agreed to accompany Gentry's son, Allen, and a load of goods down the Ohio and then along the Mississippi into Louisiana. Together, they took a cargo of corn, meat, and flour to New Orleans.

At first the two young men made their way downriver slowly, stopping several times to trade at local plantations on the way. After a brush with a group of marauding blacks who attacked them at night and tried to kill them and steal their goods, the young men made better time.

New Orleans in 1828 was far and away the largest city Lincoln had ever seen. Lincoln also received his first exposure to plantation slavery and masses of black slaves on this trip. He did not record any reaction to this first brush with what he would later consider one of the greatest of personal evils. Of course, at the time, Lincoln was scarcely nineteen years old, still forming the opinions that would one day lead him to declare, "If slavery isn't evil, nothing is."

Three years later Denton Offutt, whom Lincoln had worked for previously, hired him, his cousin John Hanks, and a friend named John D. Johnston to make the trip down the Mississippi to New Orleans again. But Offutt did not want Lincoln to take a flatboat down the Ohio to where it met the Mississippi. Rather, he wanted Lincoln and his party to take his boatload of goods down the less navigable, more treacherous Sangamon River, across central Illinois, past its mouth, and then down the Mississippi to New Orleans.

This journey proved the exact opposite of the previous one. All of the difficulty this time lay at the beginning of the trip, rather than near the end. Lincoln and company ran their flatboat aground on a milldam erected near the village of New Salem. The boat began to take on water as the crew labored to offload its cargo and float it free of the milldam.

Lincoln saved the day by coming up with the idea of drilling a hole in the bow of the boat, then offloading enough of the boat's cargo in the rear so that the stern lifted up and the water threatening to sink the boat poured through the hole in the bow. The rest of the trip was uneventful.

When Lincoln returned upriver, he took a job Offutt offered him, running a new store in New Salem, where he had almost lost his cargo. Within a year, Lincoln had opened Offutt's store and announced his intention to run for the Illinois State Legislature.

According to Lincoln, one of his reasons for running was that he knew the neighboring Sangamon River well. As such, he was the ideal candidate to advocate for internal improvements that would make that river more navigable. This in turn would make it easier for the citizens of New Salem (mostly farmers) to get their crops to market by riverboat.

He capped his announcement by taking the helm of "the splendid, upper cabin steamer *Talisman*" as she made her way up the Illinois River, past the mouth of the Sangamon, then up to Portland Landing. The whole point of the *Talisman*'s journey from Cincinnati was to prove the navigability of the Sangamon. During the trip Lincoln helped clear brush and other obstructions before the steamer's arrival in the area, then got his name in the papers as a candidate for the state legislature by piloting the boat on the last portion of her journey. Smooth political work, at that.

15 Why did Lincoln's first run for the Illinois State Legislature fail?

In 1832, a number of Abraham Lincoln's friends in the village of New Salem encouraged him to run for the Illinois State Legislature. The position required nothing (not even literacy) by way of qualification, aside from being a white male over twenty-one years of age. Those who planted the idea in the twenty-three-year-old's head included Judge Bowling Green (and you thought some professional athletes had strange names); John McNeil, a local storekeeper; Mentor Graham, New Salem's semiliterate schoolmaster; and John Stuart, who later became Lincoln's first law partner.

The presidential election of 1832 revolved around the contest between popular incumbent Andrew Jackson and his challenger, Henry Clay of Kentucky. Jackson headed Thomas Jefferson's old Democratic Republicans (the name shortened simply to "Democrats"). Clay's party called itself the Whigs, styling themselves after Britain's political party of the same name.

The British Whigs had evolved as a political party out of Parliament's battles with a series of would-be tyrannical kings. Likewise, the American Whigs frequently referred to Jackson as "King Andrew I." They hoped that their choice of name would tie in with efforts to paint Jackson as a despot.

Lincoln supported Clay and ran as a Whig. In fact, he lionized his fellow Kentuckian. He and many others in Illinois welcomed Clay's proposals for internal improvements in the West, such as new and better canals and roads, more navigable rivers, and a strong national bank to print and regulate a national currency. These national questions didn't really play much part in Illinois politics during the election of 1832, though. That came later.

Consequently, Lincoln's campaigning focused on issues that were of interest to a farming community like New Salem. For instance, Lincoln promised that the Sangamon River would be dredged and improved for riverboat navigation. This issue was very important to local farmers who were concerned about getting their crops to market.

Since cash was in short supply and land, which was plentiful, was not worth much as collateral on the Illinois frontier, banks charged high interest rates. Lincoln insisted that if elected he would do his best to prevent banks from charging Illinois farmers and businessmen high interest rates.

In retrospect, Lincoln didn't stand much chance of winning in his first bid for elective office. He had no money himself and certainly no campaign fund. Not a year previously he had been, by his own account, a "friendless, uneducated, penniless boy, working on a flatboat-at ten dollars per month." Lincoln himself thought so little of his chances in this election that he consistently hedged his bets on the point. In a campaign announcement he wrote for Springfield's *Sangamo Journal*, he made statements such as, "I was born and have ever remained in the most humble walks of life." He even wrote that if he lost, it would come as no terrible blow since he found himself "too familiar with disappoints to be very much chagrined" at the possibility of defeat.

In 1832, and before the election, Lincoln became a militiaman during the Black Hawk War with the Sauk and Fox Indian tribes, so that he could collect militia pay. This hurt his ability to campaign, but probably affected the outcome of the election very little, since even back then successful campaigning took money, which Lincoln did not have.

In the end, Lincoln placed eighth out of thirteen candidates for four seats. He was quite fond of pointing out later in life that his first foray into politics was the first and last time he "was ever beaten on a direct vote of the people." In his home precinct of New Salem, Lincoln received 277 of 300 votes cast, and that pleased him no end.

16 Why did Lincoln's dry-goods store fail?

After the Black Hawk War ended in mid-1832, Abraham Lincoln returned to New Salem. Because Denton Offutt's business had failed before Lincoln left to serve in the state militia, Lincoln came home unemployed, in debt, and with few prospects. He spent the next few months doing odd jobs and performing day labor for neighbors.

Then the Herndon brothers, who ran one of New Salem's three dry-goods stores, decided to sell out. A Black Hawk War comrade named William F. Berry bought half interest in the Herndons' business, and J. Rowan Herndon, from whom Lincoln was renting a room, offered the other half to Lincoln in return for Lincoln's signature on a promissory note. "I believed he was thoroughly honest," Herndon said, "and that impression was so strong in me I accepted his note in payment of the whole."

Nearly from the day they opened for business, Lincoln seems to have realized that his venture with Berry was doomed. They had little in the way of goods to sell and few customers. Lincoln passed his time swapping stories with friends around the cracker barrel, discussing politics and religion with the debating partners in his social set, and reading incessantly. Berry made next to no contribution to the store's operation. Rumor had it that he drank too much, and even if those rumors weren't true, Lincoln himself said of his partner that he was "a thriftless soul."

The one thing Berry did do to try to save the store was to apply for a license to sell liquor by the glass (thereby converting their business from dry-goods sales to a "grocery store," which was actually more like what we would call a tavern or a pub). The single area in which Lincoln and Berry's establishment showed a profit was in their sale of beer and whiskey. Lincoln himself did not drink, and later said that he "never kept a grocery any where in the world." (He was running for the Senate at the time, and past ownership of a liquor store was something that wouldn't have played well with voters in 1850s Illinois). What's more, the application Berry filed had a forged signature in the place where Lincoln should have signed.

The main factor contributing to the failure of Lincoln and Berry's business, though, was the fact that New Salem was not large enough to support two dry-goods stores. With the lack of roads, the poor navigability of the Sangamon River, and no railroad line on which to get their crops and wares to larger markets, by the early 1830s the citizens of New Salem began to drift to other communities with better infrastructure. Put simply, the town was dying.

One of the first casualties of this trend was Lincoln and Berry's store. Not long afterward, Berry died. Although Lincoln was not legally liable for Berry's half of the debts incurred by their failed business, he insisted on taking it on in addition to what he himself owed. For years afterward he paid on this large sum, repeatedly referring to it in a joking manner as his "national debt." Joking aside, he took it seriously enough to pay off the entire amount, though it was far from easy for him to do so.

17 Abe Lincoln: New Salem postmaster

After his dry-goods partnership with William Berry failed, Lincoln went back to working odd jobs and splitting rails for a while, until a few of his friends got him a new job as postmaster. The job didn't pay much, but together with the odd jobs he did it covered his expenses and kept him from needing to leave New Salem.

Lincoln took the post seriously, too. He was very conscientious about delivering the mail, including to families who lived well outside of town. Most of the stories about Lincoln's walking many country miles to deliver mail he stored in his stovepipe hat are true. Actually, the position of postmaster was ideal for Lincoln. It meant he got to read every newspaper that came to town for delivery, furthering his continued attempts to better himself by feeding his voracious appetite for news of the outside world.

Lincoln continued on as New Salem's postmaster until he moved to Springfield to read law as a clerk in John Stuart's offices. Up until that time, he combined the job with farm labor, surveying, and his eventual position as a state legislator, all in order to keep body and soul together, and to pay down what he referred to as his "national debt."

18 Lincoln's (brief) military "career"

In the spring of 1831, an Indian chief named Keokuk sold a large parcel of land along the eastern bank of the Mississippi River to the United States government. As a result, another Indian chief named Black Hawk and his followers lost the village site where they and their families had lived for more than 100 years. They and many other members of their tribe (the Sauk), along with their neighbors and close relatives, the Fox, retreated across the Mississippi, where they found themselves at the mercy of traditional enemies like the various bands of eastern Sioux.

In the spring of 1832, an ambitious twenty-three-year-old store clerk and candidate for the Illinois legislature named Abraham Lincoln lost his job. That same week Black Hawk and several hundred of his people, including about 500 warriors, recrossed the Mississippi and tried to take back their land.

Because he was politically ambitious and realized that a stint of military service could be helpful to his political career, and more important because he was broke, Abraham Lincoln joined the militia. What ensued for Black Hawk and his people was a lopsided tragedy. What ensued for Abraham Lincoln was a short and undistinguished military career.

On April 21, 1832, the men of Lincoln's newly sworn-in militia unit voted to elect their officers. Lincoln won handily after some of the local bully-boys made a loud show of backing him. Lincoln was so proud of having won this election that shortly before running for president he referred specifically to this honor, saying that it was "a success which gave me more pleasure than any I have had since." Not bad coming from someone who served four terms in the Illinois State Legislature, served one term in the U.S. House of Representatives, and was twice nominated for the U.S. Senate.

Lincoln spent a lot of time teaching his men to march. He never really got the hang of it though, and he loved to tell a story that illustrated this fact. According to Lincoln he had his company of new militiamen marching straight toward a fence, and he couldn't remember the command to get them to redress their lines in order to fit through the gate in that fence. He hit upon a pragmatic solution. He simply ordered the company to halt, and reform its lines on the other side of the fence.

Lincoln later said of his military service, "In the days of the Black Hawk War, I fought, bled, and came away." Later he elaborated on the fighting and bleeding parts. Lincoln joked that during his few months of service he never saw any Indians, but "I had a good many bloody struggles with the mosquetoes [*sic*]; and, although I never fainted from loss of blood, I can truly say I was often very hungry."

Lincoln re-enlisted as a private when his initial enlistment expired a few months later. By the end of that enlistment Black Hawk and his followers had lost their short-lived war, so the governor mustered Lincoln and his neighbors out of the militia. For years afterward, Lincoln told humorous stories about his stint of military duty during the Black Hawk War.

19   Abe Lincoln: Surveyor

Lincoln's position as New Salem's postmaster gave him standing in the community and excellent opportunities to network with local citizens (always important for someone with political aspirations). But it didn't pay well. When county surveyor John Calhoun mentioned he was looking for an assistant, some of the same friends who helped Lincoln get the postmaster job pressed him to accept the position.

At first Lincoln was reluctant. First of all, public positions at that time depended upon political connections. Calhoun was a prominent local Democrat. Lincoln was a Whig. Second, Lincoln knew nothing about surveying. He had less than a year of formal schooling, including some basic knowledge of math, but was ignorant of geometry. Calhoun wasn't sure Lincoln was suitable for the post.

Once Calhoun received assurances that Lincoln's politics would not keep him from doing the job expected of him as Calhoun's assistant, Lincoln set about educating himself on the subject of surveying. In very little time he was able to take on some of Calhoun's work and proved himself to be very good as a surveyor. Once he had truly mastered the science of surveying, Lincoln began to work on more advanced tasks than laying out farmers' claims. He laid out the plans for a number of central Illinois villages and hamlets, including Bath, Huron, New Boston, and Petersburg. He was also the primary surveyor for a road that ran from the Sangamon River up the hill to New Salem, and onward to the neighboring town of Jacksonville.

Between what he made as a surveyor and what he earned as postmaster, Lincoln was able to live quite comfortably. However, within a year, the notes he had signed to go into business with Berry came due, and his surveying equipment, along with his horse and saddle, were seized to pay part of his outstanding debt.

Lincoln did no surveying at all during the spring and most of the summer of 1835 until a friend named James Short bought Lincoln's surveying equipment at auction for $120 (a lot of money in 1835!) and returned them to Lincoln. For some reason, the sheriff returned Lincoln's horse to him rather than auctioning it, saying simply that it was exempt from auction. Within weeks Lincoln had gone back to surveying work, collecting the fees that helped him pay down his debts.

20 Why was Lincoln's second run for the Illinois State Legislature successful?

We know Lincoln as "Honest Abe," a truthful, upstanding moral leader of unimpeachable principles. According to our national myth, Lincoln was above the sorts of concerns that prompt us to curl our lips at today's career politicians.

Honest? Absolutely. Possessed of strong character? Definitely. But it's erroneous to assume that Abraham Lincoln was not a career politician. He was. Politics was a lifelong passion for him. He had a personality for politics, with his love of pressing the flesh and meeting people, his charm, his wit, his self-deprecating humor, and his endless supply of stories.

In many ways, Abraham Lincoln was the consummate politician because he was able to wed a strong streak of honesty with sound political instincts. His successful second run for a seat in the Illinois State Legislature is good proof of this.

Lincoln's experience as a surveyor throughout central Illinois stood him in good stead during his second run for the state legislature. He had made many friends among the overwhelmingly Democratic-leaning independent farmers of the area, and he was not above making grand gestures to gain votes. This included helping a bunch of farm hands harvest their grain.

When he heard that these men would never vote for someone who was unfamiliar with fieldwork, Lincoln shucked his coat, assured them he was their man, then led them in one circuit around the field. Lincoln's friend Rowan Herndon later said, "I don't think he Lost a vote in the Croud [*sic*]." Lincoln was smart enough to run a campaign where he said little about his Whig Party membership and his Whig principles. Instead, he chose to run on his personality, emphasizing his personal relationships with so many of the Democrat farmers in his district.

Lincoln's successful first election to the Illinois State Legislature eventually came down to a backroom political deal—one with which his posthumous mythmakers probably would never have associated his name. As was the case during his first run for the legislature, thirteen candidates were running in Lincoln's home district for four open seats. The Democrats were more concerned with defeating Lincoln's old Black Hawk War friend John Todd Stuart than with defeating Lincoln. Stuart had been positioning himself to run for national office, using his post as a Whig Party leader to expand his prestige at the expense of potential Democrat rivals.

So the Democrats offered to drop their support for two of their own candidates and concentrate on getting Lincoln elected, hoping his gaining one of the four open legislative seats would ace out Stuart. Lincoln's response to this backroom deal was at once honest, smart, and utterly political. It was also emblematic of Lincoln's emerging political style.

Lincoln went to Stuart and asked him what he thought Lincoln should do. Stuart told Lincoln to take the deal. Stuart was certain that he had enough votes to get re-elected, even with the Democrats targeting him. It turned out that Stuart was right. On August 4, 1834, Lincoln got the second-highest number of votes (1,376) among the thirteen candidates, and Stuart placed fourth, with just enough to win re-election.

So Lincoln won election to the Illinois State Legislature for the first time in part because he was a brilliant personal campaigner. But he also owed his election to the sort of backroom political deals that politicians have made in order to get and hold political power since before Rome became a republic.

21 Was Lincoln a good state legislator?

Absolutely. In fact, within a couple of years Lincoln was a leader among Whigs in the legislature. As his familiarity with the art of politics grew, so did his self-confidence, and with his self-confidence, his ability to persuade, and so on.

Lincoln's first term in the legislature (December 1, 1834, to February 13, 1835) was hardly memorable, except when chunks of plaster began to fall from the partially collapsed ceiling of the dilapidated legislative building. At the time that Lincoln entered the legislature, the state capitol was located in a tiny, remote village in southern Illinois called Vandalia. In addition to its crumbling ceiling, Vandalia had no railroad access and was tough to get to by road and river. Many other venues in Illinois were vying for the plum position of succeeding tiny, inaccessible Vandalia as the state capital.

As he gained stature in the Whig faction within the state house, Lincoln took on the leadership of the initiative to move the state capital to Springfield, a central Illinois town just down the Sangamon River from his adopted home of New Salem. It was in large part due to his stewardship of the bill approving Springfield as the new state capital that the bill passed in the House.

Lincoln was very effective at using parliamentary tricks to get his party's agenda passed, or to stymie the agenda of the rival Democratic Party. One time, trying to keep the Democrats from passing a bill the Whigs didn't want to get through, he actually convinced the other members of the Whig Party then in attendance to jump out of a window to keep from being marked as present, and thus prevent the quorum of voting members of the legislature needed to pass the bill.

Lincoln's record in the Illinois State Legislature shows that he took his position as a servant of the people seriously. During his first term he never missed a legislative session or a single committee meeting. Later, as he became more familiar with the requirements of his position, he allowed himself to be absent when other business called him away from Springfield, but he consistently ranked among the top members of the legislature in votes cast and roll calls answered.

Most importantly, Lincoln learned how to motivate, how to make deals, and how to lead. This experience stood him in good stead during his presidency. Lincoln frequently had to deal with an uncooperative Congress, and sometimes even a difficult cabinet member.

22 What did it mean to "read law" in a law office?

Shortly after Abraham Lincoln was elected to a first term in the Illinois State Legislature in 1834, he decided to become a lawyer. In 1834 there were no law schools. Anyone who wished to practice law had to pass a test (known today as a bar exam) and then pay a fee in order to be licensed to practice law in the state where he'd chosen to take that test. In order to prepare for this, young men wishing to become practicing attorneys usually followed the traditional practice of "reading law."

This meant that a young man went out and found an attorney already practicing law in the region where he, too, hoped to practice. Then he went to work for that lawyer as a law clerk, copying documents and writing up pleas, wills, and so forth. Sometimes, this job paid a fee; often it did not. The idea was that the young man in question would gain experience beneficial to his studies, and his employer/mentor's law books would be open to him.

During the time he wasn't occupied doing clerical work, the young man was expected to "read law," in other words, to sift through the available written resources that would, in turn, acquaint him with existing case law in any number of fields. Since the American legal system was based in large part on English Common Law, British law books were common sources of legal education as well. Such venerable texts as Sir William Blackstone's *Commentaries on English Civil Law* were prized possessions in many a nineteenth-century law library, and Lincoln was understandably thrilled when he found a copy of Blackstone's *Commentaries* at an auction.

As late as 1833, Lincoln had decided against studying law. He thought his education too scanty and his intelligence not enough to make up the difference between himself and other better-educated men. His election to the state legislature the following year changed all that. His old friend and Whig colleague John Todd Stuart had his own practice and offered to let Lincoln "read law" in his law office.

So Lincoln worked as a clerk in Stuart's office during his spare time up until he was admitted to the state bar in September 1836. He immediately went into partnership with Stuart, who was very busy preparing to run for Congress.

Because he was a novice, Lincoln received only one-third of the firm's profits, but because Stuart's energies were devoted elsewhere he did the lion's share of the firm's work. So Lincoln started his legal career the way many lawyers these days do: working more hours than the firm's senior partners for a lot less pay. Some things never change.

23 Ann Rutledge: The great love of Lincoln's life?

Who was Ann Rutledge? Much has been written about her, including at least two different biographies of varying accuracy. People who knew her proclaimed her everything from Abraham Lincoln's lost love to the reason he once considered suicide. The verifiable facts are a lot more ambiguous.

Here is what we do know about her. Ann Rutledge was born on January 17, 1813, near Henderson, Kentucky. She was the third of ten children born to her parents, James and Mary Rutledge. When Ann was sixteen, her father uprooted the family and moved them to southern Illinois.

Once there, James Rutledge and his partner John M. Cameron dammed the Sangamon River. They eventually founded the village of New Salem on a bluff overlooking the dam. After they had dammed the river, Rutledge and Cameron set about building a sawmill and then a gristmill. Rutledge's daughter Ann was the first female student at Mentor Graham's school in New Salem, and the only one during the first year after it opened.

Business was so good in this booming frontier town that by 1830 James Rutledge had converted his home into a tavern, and within a few years, Ann took over its management. By all accounts the customers liked her. According to her cousin James McGrady Rutledge, Ann was "a beautiful girl, and as bright as she was beautiful." Cheerful, outgoing, kindly, and a skilled seamstress, she was apparently quite a catch, and she quickly became engaged to one of Lincoln's friends, a young New Yorker named John McNeil. McNeil, whose real name was McNamar, had moved west from New York to revive the family fortunes after his father failed at business. According to Ann, McNamar changed his name because he was worried "that if the family in New York had known where he was, they would have settled down on him, and before he could have accumulated any property they would have sunk him beyond recovery."

By the time he asked Ann to marry him, McNamar was part-owner of a successful general store and had acquired a fortune worth at least $10,000. Shortly after the couple announced their engagement, McNamar left New Salem, saying that he was going to New York to bring his family out west to his land in Illinois. Ann Rutledge never saw him again.

Ann had known Abraham Lincoln since she was a schoolgirl. Once she took over the management of her father's tavern, where Lincoln lodged, she saw him more frequently. Lincoln, who could be shy and awkward with single girls his own age, took a particular shine to the smiling, plump, and bustling Ann.

This probably had something to do with her engagement. Since Ann was "spoken for," Lincoln was able to relax and enjoy her company, as he is reported to have done with many of the married women he knew. Because, as one Dr. Duncan put it, Lincoln considered Ann's engagement to be "an insurmountable barier [sic]," he didn't act stiff and formal around her. As a result, their friendship deepened.

At some point within the year after McNamar abandoned Ann, she and Lincoln came to an understanding. They agreed to become engaged, but they also decided to delay their marriage for a few important reasons. Ann felt she had to face McNamar on his return to New Salem and break the engagement, rather than allow him to return to find his betrothed wed to another man. Lincoln for his part made little money working his three jobs as surveyor, postmaster, and part-time state legislator. He worried very much about being able to support a wife. Since Lincoln intended to practice law, the two young lovers agreed to marry after Lincoln passed the bar.

Whether their marriage might have been a happy one we'll never know. Ann, so cheerful and full of life, grew ill during the summer of 1835 with what was probably typhoid fever. As she lay near death, she called Lincoln to her. They spent their last hour together alone in her sickroom. Ann's sister, Nancy, saw Lincoln leave at the end of that final visit and said later, "I can never forget how sad and broken-hearted Lincoln looked when he came out of the room from the last interview with Annie. No one knows what was said at that meeting, for they were alone together."

Ann Rutledge died a short time later, in August of 1835. She was only twenty-two. Her death seems to have shaken Lincoln to his core. The first time it rained after Ann's funeral, Lincoln told his friend Mrs. Bennett Abell "that he could not bare [sic] the idea of its raining on her grave." He rapidly sank deep into depression, but within a month of Ann's death he recovered enough to go back to work as a surveyor.

Lincoln remembered Ann for the rest of his life, though. Shortly after he was elected president, he talked about his days in New Salem with a friend named Isaac Cogdal. Cogdal asked Lincoln whether he had been in love with Ann Rutledge. "It is true," he said. "True indeed I did." And Lincoln was always specific on that point. "I loved the woman dearly and soundly: she was a handsome girl—would have made a good loving wife . . . I did honestly and truly love the girl and think often—often of her now."

He never spoke about what passed between them during their last visit together. For her part, Mary Todd, the woman who eventually became Lincoln's wife, refused altogether to believe that he had ever even been engaged to Ann Rutledge.

The death of Ann Rutledge: Proof of Lincoln's depressive personality?

Some historians have made much note of Abraham Lincoln's occasional fits of what we today call depression. Unquestionably, there were times in his life when he felt down and disheartened. His close friend and fellow Kentuckian Jake Speed once noted that Lincoln had, on at least a couple of occasions, gone to his bed and not left for an entire week.

Keep in mind, this was a man who lost a younger brother before he was five, his mother shortly thereafter, and his sister before he was twenty. He grew up doing work he hated for a father with whom he did not communicate well. He lost his first fiancée (Ann Rutledge) to a fever. After Ann Rutledge's death, he faced the hardship of having two of his four sons predecease him, and he bore the terrible burden of being president during the four bloodiest years of this country's history. This is enough to drive even the most grounded person into a funk, and furthermore, Lincoln seems to have had a family history of depression.

To our knowledge, the last time Lincoln was afflicted by what he called "the hypo" (short for hypocondriasis) was after he broke off his engagement with Mary Todd in January 1841 (the two eventually reconciled and wed in November 1842). Marriage and maturity may have helped even out Lincoln's temperament, and he never again took to his bed for anything other than sleep or illness. But was he the "saddest man" many people said they'd ever met because of anything besides his experiences? The best answer we can come up with is probably.

25 "Dueling" with James Shields

In 1842 Abraham Lincoln picked a fight with a Democrat firebrand named James Shields over a dispute about the closing of the Illinois State Bank. Shields's weak point was his vanity. He took care of his appearance, had formal manners, and considered himself a real lady-killer. On top of this, Shields had no sense of humor, which made for a dangerous combination of ingredients when Lincoln used his poison-pen letters to strike directly at the heart of Shields's narcissism. Writing under the pen name of Rebecca, a supposedly uneducated yet perceptive farmwoman, Lincoln produced several very funny letters for publication in the *Sangamo Journal*, in which he mocked Shields and his policies mercilessly.

Then Lincoln's on-again-off-again fiancée Mary Todd got into the act with her friend Julia Jaynes. The two women collaborated on their own anonymous letter, claiming that Shields now intended to marry Rebecca. Shields exploded.

He furiously demanded that the editor of the *Journal* reveal the name of the persons writing these letters about him. Lincoln agreed to allow his name to be mentioned in association with all of the letters in question. Shields demanded "a full, positive and absolute retraction of all offensive allusions used by you in these communications."

Shields and Lincoln knew each other before this dustup, and Lincoln seems to have been aware of the likely result of his refusal to comply with the demands made in Shields's note. Although Shields mentioned nothing about a duel, Lincoln's immediate response was to rule one out, because he himself was "wholly opposed to dueling, and would do anything to avoid it that might not degrade him in the estimation of himself and his friends."

Unfortunately, Lincoln didn't leave it at that, but made the mistake of adding his mercurial friend Elias H. Merryman into the mix. When Lincoln consulted Merryman for advice, the hotheaded young doctor insisted Lincoln should not apologize. Lincoln allowed Merryman to sway him because the note Shields had sent him was full of "so much assumption of facts, and so much of menace." It was better to fight a duel with Shields than to willingly suffer "such *degradation.*"

This is when things really started to heat up. Shields named his second (General John D. Whiteside, who had delivered the initial letter to Lincoln), and Lincoln his (Merryman, of course). Because Shields had challenged him, Lincoln got to choose the weapons the two men would use. He chose broadswords, obviously hoping to take advantage of his greater height and longer reach. Since dueling was illegal in Illinois, the two men agreed to meet in Missouri.

On September 22, 1842, Lincoln and Shields met at the agreed-upon place across the Mississippi River from Alton, Illinois. Both men were accompanied by their seconds, along with several other friends. Right before the duel started, two men intervened. One, John J. Hardin, was Mary Todd's cousin and Lincoln's Whig ally. The other, Dr. R. W. English, was (like Hardin) a good friend of both Lincoln and Shields.

Together these two managed to defuse the situation. They convinced Shields to retract what he had said in his first letter to Lincoln. In return, Lincoln agreed that he never intended to impugn Shields's "personal or private character or standing . . . as a man or a gentleman," saying that he intended the letters in question to be "solely for political effect."

In retrospect, both men were lucky they allowed cooler heads to prevail in this matter. Lincoln of course went on to be a U.S. congressman and later president of the United States. By the time he died in 1879, Shields was the only man ever to hold a U.S. Senate seat from three different states (Illinois, Minnesota, and Missouri) and was a distinguished veteran of the Civil War, in which he served as a brigadier general.

After this crisis was averted, Lincoln was so appalled by his behavior he discussed it with Mary, and they agreed never to talk about it or bring it up to each other or anyone else again. Years later, Lincoln still flushed with color at the mere mention of his near duel.

Lincoln took a powerful lesson away from this whole affair: He realized there were potentially harmful consequences from playing the negative politics of planting anonymous letters in prominent newspapers. He had been dabbling in this long-accepted political practice since his first term in the state legislature, but he resolved never to do so again. He realized his wicked sense of humor, when not properly reined in, could do serious harm to others' feelings, and that realization appalled him.

Interestingly enough, it is Shields's statue that represents Illinois (the "Land of Lincoln," if state automobile license plates count for anything) in Washington, D.C.'s National Statuary Hall. Apparently the people of Illinois figured a memorial dominating one end of the Mall in the capital city was enough for their favorite son.

26 Lincoln's personal relationships

In many ways our most famous president is a cipher, especially when it comes to his personal relationships. So outwardly charming, so personally reserved, so often masking his personal feelings behind a barrage of one-liners, Lincoln simply was not the sort of man given to public displays of emotion.

His personal relationships reflect this. At one time or another, many people felt close to Lincoln, among them his wife, Mary, his law partner William H. Herndon, his friend Joshua Speed, and any number of political allies, including Secretary of State William Seward and Secretary of War Edwin M. Stanton.

Another Mary, Mary Owens, was at one time engaged to Lincoln, but broke off their nuptials after Lincoln began to show ambivalence toward her. Then there was Ann Rutledge, with whom Lincoln may or may not have had an "understanding," depending upon how you look at the record. How close Lincoln felt to any of them is open to speculation, because Abraham Lincoln was one of the most private men ever to hold the national spotlight.

In fact, Lincoln's sphinx-like nature has led to periodic speculation that his friendships with several of his male friends were more than friendships, that our sixteenth president was a homosexual. Chief among those singled out for a likely gay relationship with Lincoln was Springfield storekeeper Joshua Speed. Lincoln's official biographers (and his former personal secretaries) John Hay and John G. Nicolay called Speed "the only—as he was certainly the last—intimate friend that Lincoln ever had."

Speed rented one side of his bed to the newly arrived Lincoln shortly after the two met in Springfield. The arrangement lasted for four years, until Speed moved home to his family's Kentucky plantation and got married shortly afterward.

Although the idea of two grown unmarried men not related by blood sharing a bed might raise any number of eyebrows today, the practice was commonplace on the nineteenth-century American frontier, where beds were luxuries. In fact, for two of the four years that Lincoln and Speed shared a bed, Speed also rented out part of the room to two other unmarried young men. Needless to say, Speed's room was hardly a love nest, but it was quite a moneymaker for the young landlord.

After Speed, there are others who have aroused the interest of writers: for instance, take Elmer Ellsworth, a young protégé of Lincoln's during the late 1850s. Lincoln was devastated when Ellsworth was killed early in the Civil War. Then there's Pennsylvania Militia Captain David Derickson, Lincoln's personal bodyguard, who was rumored to have slept in the same bed with Lincoln when Mrs. Lincoln was out of town.

Unfortunately for those interested in painting Lincoln as gay, there is precious little proof to go along with the rumors, the raised eyebrows, and the innuendos. The fact is, Lincoln married and fathered numerous children, as did both Speed and Derickson. Likewise, when he died, Ellsworth was engaged to a woman with whom he appears to have been passionately in love. Yet, proponents of this theory have, in turn, shrugged this off by pointing out that plenty of gay men have sired offspring, and have even had long marriages.

Yet others point to the youthful Lincoln's comic poem commemorating the "wedding-bed prank" (see number 10), which deals in part with a supposed gay marriage. A cursory examination of this text reveals it to be a lampoon, not a wistful tribute to the love-which-dare-not-speak-its-name. However, this type of claim is nearly impossible to disprove, in part because it's so difficult to prove.

As it stands, what we know about Abraham Lincoln from the visible record, including his correspondence, is that he was a loving father, a frequently inattentive husband who flirted shamelessly with his wife via letter during her absences, usually once he'd had a chance to miss her, and intimate friends with no one after he and Joshua Speed grew apart. We cannot say definitively what his sexual orientation was, but there doesn't seem to be much evidence to support the claim that he was gay.

Part 2

The Middle Years:
Lincoln in Springfield

Why did Abraham Lincoln move to Springfield in the first place? And once there, why did he stay? After a long struggle against the poverty he experienced during his youth, Lincoln's life changed a great deal as a result of his lengthy residence in Springfield. Not only did he meet and fall in love with Mary Todd, he became a successful lawyer, too. How did the years he spent in Springfield help to shape the man who went on to become our greatest president? In this section, you'll find the answers to this and other fascinating questions about Lincoln's life.

27 Re-election to the Illinois State Legislature

Lincoln was not only re-elected to the Illinois State House, he was re-elected three consecutive times after his initial victory in 1834. He served in the state legislature a total of six years, from 1835 to 1841.

By 1841 Lincoln had established himself as a successful attorney based out of Springfield and no longer felt challenged by his position in the Illinois State House. His law partnership with John Todd Stuart had ended by mutual (and amicable) decision that same year, because Stuart was so busy with his work as a U.S. congressman. At the end of his last term in the state legislature, Lincoln was just settling into a profitable partnership with the successful Stephen T. Logan.

Lincoln had his eye set on eventually running for Stuart's seat in Congress, and that final consideration helped him to decide not to run for state office again. So Lincoln began devoting all his energies to trying cases, earning fees, and building up as much political goodwill as possible in central Illinois (the Eighth Congressional District). He did the latter by tirelessly campaigning for other Whig candidates and by networking with Whig Party members and government officials throughout the state. These moves paid off in 1846, when Abraham Lincoln won election to serve in the Thirtieth United States Congress.

28 What was the "Long Nine"?

The phrase "the Long Nine" referred to the Sangamon County delegation in the 1836–37 state legislative session. The seven representatives and two senators were called the Long Nine because all of them were extremely tall men. In a time when the average adult male could expect to reach a height of perhaps five feet six, many of the members of the Sangamon delegation were well over six feet.

The Long Nine were also remarkable because they were fairly united on two objectives: to support Springfield as the potential state capital and to support such internal improvements as river dredging, bridge building, construction and expansion of rail lines, and so on. By 1836 Lincoln had proven himself a conscientious public servant and had become a seasoned legislator. By virtue of both his experience and his ability, he became their unquestioned floor leader.

The Long Nine were successful in getting the legislature to approve the relocation of the state capital to Springfield, and saw initial success in their attempts to get sweeping internal improvement projects passed throughout the state. Then the Panic of 1837 (brought on in large part by the ruinous economic policies of former President Andrew Jackson) struck in March of that year. It so completely wrecked state finances that progress on many of the internal improvements the Long Nine had worked to get passed simply stopped well before completion because state money had dried up.

So the famous Long Nine's record was split. On the one hand, they got the capital of Illinois moved to Springfield. On the other hand (and through no fault of their own), they gained no ground on the question of hoped-for internal improvements in both their district and in the state of Illinois.

29 What firm did Lincoln first work for as a lawyer?

After he was licensed to practice law in Illinois, Lincoln went to work for the lawyer who had allowed him to read law in his office, John Todd Stuart. Lincoln and Stuart were partners from 1837 until 1841. During most of that time Lincoln handled the lion's share of the business because Stuart was either busy running for Congress or away serving in Congress.

In 1841 Lincoln and Stuart broke up their partnership because Stuart intended to spend even more time in Washington, D.C., planning to run for Congress again. Lincoln went into practice with Stephen T. Logan, a more established, well-educated lawyer. Although the firm of Logan & Lincoln brought in more money in the average month than the firm of Stuart & Lincoln had, Lincoln himself made less than he had with Stuart because of the partnership agreement he had signed with Logan.

Lincoln worked diligently for the firm from 1841 until he and Logan amicably dissolved their partnership in late 1844. Both men had designs on running for the same seat in Congress, and it would have been awkward to do so while still business partners.

In December of that year, Lincoln formed a partnership with young William H. Herndon, who had read law in the offices of Logan & Lincoln and only recently passed the bar exam. Their partnership lasted for the rest of Lincoln's life. Both times he left Springfield for public service in Washington, D.C. (for a seat in Congress in 1847 and for the presidency in 1861), Lincoln insisted that the law offices of Lincoln & Herndon remain open.

What did it mean to be a "circuit rider" on the Illinois State Court?

On the Illinois frontier in the early and mid–nineteenth century, most townships and villages did not have their own local court system. The state established a circuit court system to fill this vacuum.

The Illinois Circuit Court worked like this: Every spring and fall, a justice of the state court would embark on a "circuit" of the district for which he was specifically responsible. The court's eighth district (where Lincoln practiced) included all of central Illinois from the Indiana border in the east to the Mississippi River in the west, and the circuit court route took about ten weeks. Accompanying the judge were many lawyers from Springfield who supplemented their incomes by following the court, picking up fees in every town and village along the way.

The small-town attorneys who hired these traveling lawyers were usually quite eager to have experienced courtroom attorneys try cases for them. Springfield lawyers like Lincoln (who made the circuit twice a year for a number of years) thus spent almost half the calendar year away from hearth and home.

The caravan that accompanied the circuit court judge from town to town was almost like a circus troupe. Most of the lawyers made the circuit court rounds in a buggy or a wagon.

Because the state's treasury had no money for road building and improvement, the roads the circuit court caravan traveled along weren't much better than goat paths. Rivers proved particularly daunting because there were so few bridges crossing them. Many times the judge riding the circuit would ask Lincoln, as the tallest man among them, to test a potential fording place. The judge figured if Lincoln could wade across, then their wagons and buggies would be able to cross, too.

Unfortunately, the accommodations were just as primitive as the road system. Sometimes twenty men would crowd into one single room at the village inn. Despite the inconveniences, in the evenings there was fun to be had— people played games, swapped stories, and bet on just about anything they could think of. True to his outgoing nature, Lincoln was always right in the middle of it all.

Lincoln did not bother to hide his love for these ten-week jaunts away from home. A naturally gifted politician, he was always ready to make a favorable impression on new people and to strengthen existing relationships. Since it covered the Eighth Congressional District of Illinois, running with the circuit court got Lincoln's name out there in front of the voters who would one day send him to his only term in the U.S. Congress.

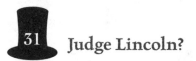

31 Judge Lincoln?

When the presiding circuit court judge, David Davis, was ill or otherwise indisposed, he would ask Lincoln to substitute for him by taking the bench and ruling as a judge pro tempore ("temporary" judge). Davis had no real authority to do this, and Lincoln's license to practice law hardly qualified him to act as a justice of the court. The only way Lincoln could legally perform a judge's duties was if everyone involved in both sides of the case in question agreed to his doing so.

Lincoln had earned such a strong reputation for honesty and fair play that most people didn't see a problem with him acting as Davis's temporary fill-in. Nevertheless, on appeal, a higher court reversed several of Lincoln's decisions. Two of them alone were overturned precisely because of the novelty of his substituting for Davis in the first place.

Lincoln presided over one particular case in which a farmer named Hartsfeller brought suit against his neighbor, another farmer named Trowbridge. Trowbridge had leased part of his land to Hartsfeller so Hartsfeller could grow corn. Trowbridge had instructed Harstfeller that under no circumstances was he to store the corn on Trowbridge's property once he'd harvested it.

Hartsfeller ignored this warning and stored the corn on one corner of Trowbridge's farm, anyway. So Trowbridge decided to teach his neighbor a lesson: He built a fence all around his farm and released his cattle into this new pasture. The cattle predictably devoured Harstfeller's corn, and Hartsfeller sued Trowbridge for damage to his property.

During this trial, Lincoln asked several pointed questions, including this one directed at Trowbridge: "And you say you went over and fenced the corn after you asked him not to crib it on your land?" When Trowbridge acknowledged that he had, Lincoln ruled in his favor. This sort of no-nonsense frontier wisdom made Lincoln a desirable choice when Judge Davis needed someone to cover for him.

32 Four jobs at one time

The year 1837 was a crossroads for Lincoln. In September of the previous year, the state of Illinois had licensed Lincoln to practice law. Before he was admitted to the bar in March of 1837 and actually began to work as an attorney, Lincoln made ends meet by working as postmaster of New Salem, as a surveyor, and as a state legislator.

But by the end of 1837, Lincoln had culled his four different paying positions down to two.

Because he'd only worked as a postmaster and surveyor to support himself while he established his position as a state legislator and then as a lawyer, he left those jobs without much regret. What's more, he was going into partnership with John Todd Stuart, which meant he had to move to Springfield. Obviously,

Lincoln couldn't deliver New Salem's mail from Springfield, so his days at the New Salem post office were already numbered.

It was better that he left the New Salem post office, anyway: It was just months from being closed because New Salem was dying a slow death. As for the surveying work, although it had been a pretty good moneymaker for Lincoln, it was a physically demanding job. Lincoln much preferred practicing law, and he was perfectly happy to quit surveying for good.

On April 15, 1837, just about a month after the Illinois State Bar Association admitted him to law practice, Lincoln said goodbye to his many friends in New Salem. Then he moved to Springfield, his political career and his destiny all waiting.

33 The real reasons for Lincoln's move to Springfield

As mentioned in the previous point, Abraham Lincoln left New Salem for Springfield in 1837. He had a number of reasons to move away from the only home he had known since leaving his father's house six years before.

In 1836 Lincoln was licensed to practice law, and once the legislative session of 1836–37 ended in late January of 1837, Lincoln returned to New Salem and began to prepare for admission to the state bar. Lincoln knew he would have to leave New Salem if he hoped to practice law successfully. With no good roads, poor river passage, and no rail line linking them to the population centers in the north of the state and west across the Mississippi River, New Salem's citizens had no way of getting their goods to these markets in a timely and profitable manner. The village, bustling and full of potential when Lincoln made it his home in 1831, had begun to lose residents, most of whom moved just down the road to Springfield.

So when Lincoln's old friend John Todd Stuart recommended Lincoln relocate permanently to Springfield to join his law practice, it was just one more reason in a sea of many such reasons to move. On April 15, 1837, Lincoln did just that.

34 Who was the "other Mary" in Lincoln's life?

In New Salem, Illinois, sometime during 1833, Abraham Lincoln met an attractive, dark-haired, dark-eyed young lady named Mary. From a prominent Kentucky family, she had come to Illinois to visit her sister, who had married a local man. After she returned home to Kentucky, folks heard Lincoln say, "If ever that girl comes back to New Salem, I am going to marry her."

In 1841, now settled in Springfield, Abraham Lincoln did court an attractive, dark-haired, dark-eyed young lady named Mary, who hailed from Kentucky. She had met him while visiting a married sister who lived in the area, but she was not the same woman described above. The Mary that Lincoln met and courted in 1833 was Mary Owens. The second Mary was Mary Todd, who later became Lincoln's wife.

Mary Owens was the younger sister of Lincoln's friend Mrs. Bennett Abell. Those who knew Mary Owens said she was "very intellectual" and "well educated." Apparently, she was also outgoing, friendly, and charming, with flashing white teeth and a pale complexion (a sign of beauty in the nineteenth century) to go with her black hair and dark eyes. Lincoln was quite taken with her.

When "that girl" returned to New Salem a couple of years later (after Ann Rutledge's death), Lincoln began to court her. Mary returned his affection initially, but she soon became concerned about how different their upbringings had been. At one point, she wrote in a letter to a friend, "His training had been different from mine; hence there was not that congeniality which would otherwise have existed."

To put it bluntly, Mary was a Kentucky belle, and she was used to genteel company. Abraham Lincoln was a bit of an oaf. Sure, he was a kindhearted, well-meaning, amusing oaf, but he didn't have the sort of polished manners Mary was accustomed to. She was not the only one with doubts, though. Like so many young men, Lincoln began to suspect that his paramour was a bit too eager to accept his offer of courtship. At first, he hardly dared to hope that someone he found so attractive would be interested in him. Within days, however, he found himself wondering just why she *was* with him—yet another manifestation of his insecurity.

And while she was busy noticing his lack of manners, he started thinking she wasn't just "pleasingly plump," she was outright fat. It seems Lincoln was always attracted to plump women (Ann Rutledge and Mary Todd were both "healthy girls" in this respect). But in the eyes of Lincoln, apparently, Mary Owens had gone past that point. Clearly, they both had doubts. By mid-1836, Lincoln began trying to get out of their unofficial, yet binding "understanding."

Once he moved to Springfield, Lincoln wrote to her, saying that she would probably want to break things off with him since he was poor and there were so many in Springfield who made a great show of their wealth. Because Mary was from a well-to-do family, he told her, it "would be your doom to see it without sharing in it." Later, he put things more bluntly: "You would have to be poor without the means of hiding your poverty."

Since these reports weren't enough to dissuade her from marrying him, Lincoln had to take things further: He pretty much told her that she would be happier if he broke off with her. Rubbing salt further into an open wound, he went on, "I now say, that you can now drop the subject [of marriage], dismiss your thoughts (if you ever had any) from me forever, and leave this letter unanswered, without calling forth one accusing murmer [sic] from me."

As if he hadn't already said enough, he then proposed marriage! "I am willing, and even anxious to bind you faster, if I can be convinced that it will, in all considerable degree, add to your happiness."

Mary Owens probably thought he was crazy at this point, and she refused him—several times. Lincoln was surprised by how panicked he became: "My vanity is deeply wounded . . . that she whom I had taught myself to believe no body else would have, had actually rejected me with all my fancied greatness," he said. He began to see their relationship as something altogether different from what he believed it to be while so earnestly trying to end it.

Consumed with second thoughts, he tried to win Mary Owens back, but that ship had sailed. After he'd had some time to gain perspective on the matter, Lincoln admitted he had been "really a little in love with her." Eventually, his melancholy over yet another love lost dissolved into relief as he put the whole thing behind him.

That is until he met Mary Todd, another Kentucky belle in Illinois visiting a well-to-do and well-married sister. This outgoing, vivacious, plump little woman also complained about Lincoln's inattention (Lincoln was never a demonstrative man), and they too broke off their courtship at one point. Eventually, it took the threat of a duel to rekindle the sparks between them.

35 How Lincoln got Mary Todd to marry him

In life, things sometimes have a peculiar way of repeating themselves. Years earlier, Abraham Lincoln had gotten cold feet with another Kentucky belle named Mary Owens, and it happened again once he had an "understanding" with his sweetheart, Kentucky-born child of privilege, Mary Todd. And just as he had with Mary Owens, he also worked hard to break off this engagement.

Here, too, he was initially successful. Following his pattern with the previous Mary, once he'd wiggled his way out of his engagement with Mary Todd, Lincoln again panicked and tried to win his former fiancée back. Fortunately for Lincoln, while Mary Owens had repeatedly rebuffed his attempts to woo her back, Mary Todd eventually relented.

How did he do it? In time-honored fashion, Lincoln won Mary Todd's heart back because he was willing to fight over her.

In 1842, Lincoln got into a political quarrel with Illinois State Auditor James Shields (a rising star in the Illinois Democratic Party and future U.S. senator from Illinois, Minnesota, and Missouri). Lincoln had written a series of anonymous letters published in Whig newspapers intending to ridicule Shields because of a quarrel over state banking practices. Unfortunately, Shields had no sense of humor, and he became obsessed with finding out who had written the offending letters.

Lincoln had written all but the last of the letters in question, a clumsily written missive that made fun of Shields's overly formal manners and his belief that he was irresistible to women. However, he insisted on taking the blame for that one as well.

By taking responsibility for a letter he did not write, Lincoln was trying to protect his former fiancée, Mary Todd. She and Lincoln had broken off their engagement in January of 1841, but had become friendly again within a year. An ardent Whig with an active interest in politics (two things that had originally drawn Lincoln to her), Mary Todd had been impressed with the letters Lincoln wrote (he let her in on the secret). And so, together with her close friend Julia Jayne, Mary had written the letter that offended Shields the most, the one that galvanized him into action.

When Shields started slinging insults back at Lincoln, Lincoln allowed himself to be talked into refusing to respond or apologize. Next thing you know, the two had set a date and a site for a duel.

Thankfully, cooler heads prevailed on the morning of the duel, and both men were persuaded to retract the insulting things they had said and written about each other. Crisis thus averted, the duel served as a catalyst, once again uniting Lincoln and Mary Todd. Within weeks the two were again engaged. Given that their previous breakup had been quite public in nature, the two kept their second engagement a secret, especially since Mary's sister and brother-in-law, Mr. and Mrs. Ninian Edwards, weren't too fond of Lincoln after the way things had ended the first time around. Mary Todd didn't tell her sister she was getting married until the day of the wedding!

On November 4, 1842, Lincoln married Mary Todd with very little planning. His best man, a friend named James H. Matheny, also didn't know about the wedding plans until the day of the wedding. Later, Matheny recalled that Lincoln "looked and acted as if he were going to the slaughter" that day—not an altogether unique male response to impending matrimony.

36 Was Lincoln's marriage to Mary Todd a happy one?

Like many couples, the Lincolns had their share of marital problems. For one thing, they were not ideally suited to each other temperamentally speaking. Mary was outgoing, a genuine talker, who prattled on gaily in social situations. Emotional, loving, and physically demonstrative, she had a deep and abiding need for both attention and affection. She got little of either from her husband.

For his part, Lincoln was moody, introspective, and frequently withdrawn. His "rich interior life" precluded the sort of openly emotional intensity that Mary displayed and craved in return. These ingredients were a recipe for strife.

Any married couple will spend a fair amount of their first year together fighting, simply because they are learning to live together. The Lincolns sure did their share. When they fought, it usually had something to do with Lincoln ignoring his wife.

The Lincolns had their first child within a year of being married, and Mary spent most of her days cooped up in the room they rented above a Springfield tavern with her young son, Robert, followed a few years later by Eddie, who was often sick. Although this former belle was brought up with servants and was unaccustomed to the labor required to run a household on the Illinois frontier, she adapted without complaint. She cleaned, cooked, did laundry, and took care of the children while her husband worked on his law practice. When Lincoln was at home in the evenings and Mary needed conversation with another adult, she got little in return. Instead of chatting with his wife, Lincoln preferred to sit by the fire and read. She took this well too—she was devoted to him, and she knew, deep down, that he returned the sentiment.

However, Mary Todd Lincoln had her limits, and when she reached them, she tended to explode. Take one particular evening when she repeatedly asked Lincoln to tend to the living room fire because she was tied up dealing with the children. Lincoln was so absorbed in a book that her requests didn't register, and he let the fire go out. Mary was so frustrated that she picked up a piece of firewood and hit him on the head with it.

Although they did hit a few rough patches like this one, fortunately, they were few and far between. Mary was always proud of her husband, and it showed. And even though he was frequently uncomfortable with her emotional displays and her irresponsible spending, Lincoln loved his wife, too.

He sometimes took her for granted, though—like when he was in Washington, D.C., serving in the U.S. Congress. Although he had initially brought Mary and the boys to Washington with him, he eventually sent them back to Illinois. At first he was so busy with his duties as a congressman that he barely noticed his wife's absence. At length, however, he began to miss the woman he had been so quick to ship back home. His letters to her during this time period were frequent, loving, and flirtatious—so unlike Abraham Lincoln's usually sober letter writing!

Like all couples, the Lincolns did have bigger problems, including Mary's extended mourning for their son Willie when he died in the White House. Her outbursts were so over the top, Lincoln felt compelled to tell her that if she couldn't get control of her emotions, he might be forced to send her to an asylum (a threat their son Robert eventually made good on, due to his mother's increasingly erratic behavior during her later years).

In the end, though, they truly did love each other. When she died in the mid-1880s, Mary Lincoln was still wearing the ring her husband gave her in 1842, with the legend "Love Is Eternal" inscribed in it.

 ## 37 Was Mary Todd Lincoln crazy?

The short answer is probably not. Of course, there is evidence to support the contention. Mary Todd Lincoln, outgoing, vivacious, and definitely what we today call a type A personality, was unquestionably high-strung. She was known to have brained her husband with a piece of firewood on one occasion, and once, sometime in the early 1850s, she even chased him down a Springfield street brandishing a butcher knife—or a broomstick. Accounts vary.

Mary Todd Lincoln was also capricious, moody, and terribly irresponsible when it came to money matters. It is possible that she was bipolar. Some historians also believe that she suffered from undiagnosed and untreated diabetes in her later years.

She was given to extreme displays of emotion, too. As already mentioned in number 36, when her third son, Willie, died at the White House in 1862, she carried on in extravagant mourning for such a long period that her exasperated husband told her if she didn't curtail herself, she might find herself committed to an insane asylum. After Lincoln's murder in 1865, she did not leave the White

House for five weeks, and when she finally embarked for Chicago in May of that year she was so heavily decked out in widow's weeds that no one who saw her could recognize her under all those black veils.

Her health steadily deteriorated and her behavior became more and more erratic after she left the White House. Her eldest son, Robert, thought she never recovered from a blow to the head received in a fall from her carriage sometime during the early 1860s. As she began to behave more and more oddly (including paying hotel maids to spend the night in her hotel room with her because of her overwhelming fear of being alone), her son became increasingly exasperated.

Finally, overwrought by her heedless spending and emotional outbursts, Robert Todd Lincoln began legal proceedings in May 1875 to have his mother declared legally insane. He testified at her hearing (understandably, she never really forgave him for that) and convinced a judge and jury that his mother was mentally ill. The court committed her to Bellevue, a sanitarium in Batavia, Illinois, which catered to wealthy women with mild forms of mental illness.

Mary Todd Lincoln had her own suite of rooms separate from other patients, and she took her meals alone. Robert visited her weekly, although their relationship was tense. (They remained estranged until a partial reconciliation shortly before her death in 1882.) Her stay at Bellevue lasted only four months because she was able to convince another jury that she was once again mentally stable.

Mary Todd Lincoln was irresponsible, moody, eccentric, and extravagant— definitely what we would call "high maintenance" today. Emotionally unstable?

Likely. But insane? According to the state of Illinois, the answer is yes. Bear in mind, though, a nineteenth-century court of law determined this, and that's a far cry from any conclusion modern medicine might have drawn.

38 The Lincolns' early domestic life

Anyone who's been married any length of time can attest that every marriage goes through an adjustment period right at the beginning. People have to learn to live with each other and not to let their partner's annoying little quirks drive them to the brink of homicide.

The Lincolns themselves were no exception to this rule. Abraham was taciturn and frequently so introverted he'd go a whole evening without speaking to his wife. (Mary Todd Lincoln said of her husband years later that he "was *not* a demonstrative man, when he felt most deeply, he expressed the least.") For her part, Mary was a bustling, outgoing, cheerful, high-strung Kentucky belle used to a life of privilege, including servants to wait on her. To say that moving first from her father's Kentucky plantation to the Springfield home of her well-to-do sister Elizabeth Edwards and then into a single room above a tavern required some getting used to on Mary's part would be something of an understatement.

Yet move she did. To her credit, Mary resolved not to complain about their one-room accommodations. She knew that her husband was only just beginning to make money as an attorney, and things would not be easy at first. In light of Mary's temperament and extravagant ways, it is interesting to note that she seems to have been successful in honoring her resolution.

The Lincolns' living conditions really got too close for comfort with the arrival of their first child, Robert, on August 1, 1843, almost exactly nine months after his parents were married. Now, not only was Mary cooped up all day while Abraham made a living in his law offices or went away for weeks at a time on the court circuit, she was alone with an infant. Since they couldn't afford to hire anyone to help with raising young Robert, this did nothing to improve her disposition. Add her husband's undemonstrative nature on top of all this, and it was like sparks to a powder keg.

When those sparks flew, the battle tended to be one-sided. Lincoln loved his wife and saw her temperament as something to be endured rather than contended with. By most accounts, he did not fight back when his wife lashed out at him (usually with good reason).

Things improved somewhat for the Lincolns when they were able to move to a rented three-room house during the autumn of 1843. A generous allowance from Mary's father also helped. (He visited them that Christmas and was so moved by the meagerness of their existence that he arranged to send Mary $120 per year for the remainder of his life.) Mary was supposed to use that allowance for household expenses, including hiring a maid to help with the cooking, cleaning, and childrearing. This helped to ease the tension in the house, and when Abraham and Mary actually bought their own home the following year, again, tensions eased a bit between them. Still, their marriage was never what most people would call "harmonious."

39 How many homes did Lincoln own in his lifetime?

Although Lincoln lived everywhere from a half-face camp three-sided lean-to in Kentucky to the White House itself, he only ever owned one house. In 1844, he bought a house on the corner of Jackson and Eighth streets in Springfield from the Reverend Charles Dresser.

It was a small house, little more than a two-bedroom cottage, made all the smaller with the addition of the Lincolns' second son, Edward Baker Lincoln, in 1846. By 1856, it was far too small for the Lincolns' needs, and Mary set about renovating it, using some money she made after selling land her father had given her in 1844.

She added an entire second floor to the house: adjoining bedrooms for her husband and herself (in the finest Victorian fashion), a room for Robert, and one for their two younger sons, Willie and Tad, to share. There was also a maid's quarters and an impressive guest room at the rear of the second-floor hallway.

Mary discussed the renovation with her husband before he went away on the Illinois Circuit Court route. Upon returning home, he approached a neighbor and joked that he had become lost. He could have sworn that his home was right next door, but it certainly wasn't the grand affair he saw before him.

The joke backfired. Local gossip quickly spread the word that extravagant Mary Todd Lincoln had renovated their house without consulting her husband!

40 1846: Lincoln's election to the U.S. House of Representatives

In March of 1846, Abraham Lincoln became the only Whig congressman from the otherwise solidly Democratic state of Illinois. He succeeded a friend named Edward D. Baker (after whom he named his second son) in the Illinois Seventh Congressional District, located in the center of the state.

Lincoln had campaigned hard for Baker in 1844, and in return Baker promised to limit himself to a single term in the U.S. House of Representatives. (Lincoln echoed this promise in return for Whig Party support in his own 1846 campaign.) Lincoln's election was nearly a foregone conclusion once he had succeeded in gaining the Whig nomination. The nomination itself was another story.

The man who held the Illinois Seventh Congressional District seat in the U.S. House before Edward D. Baker was John J. Hardin, a prominent Whig from Jackson, Illinois. Hardin was one of the two men whose intercession had kept Lincoln from fighting that duel with James Shields a few years earlier (see number 25).

Hardin had enjoyed the term he'd served in Congress (1843–45) and wanted to run again in 1846, despite the Whig tradition in Illinois that congressmen limit themselves to a single term. So he decided to challenge Lincoln for the Whig nomination in 1846.

Lincoln was livid. It was all he could do to hold himself together and not lash out furiously at his old friend Hardin. Instead, he was the picture of control, duking it out with Hardin for over six months. Hardin and his supporters even attempted to nominate Lincoln for governor, a dodge intended to get Lincoln out of the way (no Whig could win the governor's mansion in a state as ardently Democratic as Illinois).

When Hardin repeatedly claimed that Lincoln was manipulating the convention system to his advantage, Lincoln adamantly refused to make any response at all. He told his longtime friend, *Tazewell Whig* editor Benjamin F. James that "it will be *just all we can do*, to keep out of a quarrel—and I am resolved to do my part to keep the peace." This was more than solid citizenship. Lincoln knew he had nothing to gain by allowing himself to be drawn into a war of words with someone who was losing to him in the polls. On the other hand, if he let his mouth step ahead of him, he could potentially lose the nomination. Lincoln further insisted that Hardin not be the victim of the sort of smear campaign so common to nineteenth-century politics. Hardin, he said, was "talented, energetic, usually generous, and magnanimous."

Because Lincoln had worked the circuit court route, he had built himself a formidable support base indeed, and so Hardin tried to get Lincoln to forgo the formal nomination process. Hardin advocated that every Whig who wished to run for a particular office could simply stand for that office. Since this did Lincoln no good, he declined, saying he was "entirely satisfied with the old system under which you [Hardin] and [Edward D.] Baker were successively nominated and elected to congress."

Once it became clear to Hardin that he couldn't successfully challenge Lincoln for the Whig nomination, he abruptly dropped out of the race and took a commission in the army. He headed for the Texas borderlands, where General Zachary Taylor's troops were readying for war with Mexico.

With Hardin out of the way, Lincoln handily secured the Whig nomination, and he set about campaigning against his Democratic opponent, a popular circuit-riding Methodist preacher named Peter Cartwright. Cartwright turned out to be an abysmal campaigner. Desperate to make inroads in Lincoln's popularity, Cartwright played up Lincoln's lack of affiliation with any organized church, hinting that he might be an infidel or, worse, an atheist.

Lincoln answered this terribly serious accusation by saying that he was "not a member of any Christian Church," but he was no atheist. Further, he would never "support a man for office, whom I knew to be an open enemy of, and scoffer at, religion."

As it turned out, Cartwright had good reason to be desperate. On August 3, 1846, Lincoln carried the Illinois Seventh Congressional District with a record majority of votes.

Was the greatest war president in American history actually antiwar?

41

Doctoral theses and whole libraries of books have been dedicated to the question of how our sixteenth president felt about war. During his tenure in the White House, Lincoln came out bluntly as being against war, except as a last resort.

How did he feel before he became chief executive, though? His record in the U.S. Congress during the last year of the Mexican War reveals a lot about Lincoln's feelings regarding war in general. If Lincoln ever wrote anything about the question of Texan independence from Mexico, it has not survived intact. However, in light of his referring to Mexicans as "greasers," it's likely that he approved of Texan independence.

Statehood for Texas was quite another matter. In America during the first sixty years of the nineteenth century, the terms "expansionism" and "slavery" were inextricably intertwined. Many Southerners (including nearly all of the South's congressional leadership) equated the survival of Southern culture with the preservation of the institution of slavery. In turn, what Southerners called their "peculiar (as in "unique") institution" required the ability to expand geographically to remain viable. Thus, if Northern political interests were successful in blocking the expansion of the Old South, slavery and the traditional Southern life would die a twin death.

Lincoln had a lifelong aversion to the practice of slavery, and its attachment to territorial expansionism was not lost on him. In light of this, Lincoln's 1844 remark upon hearing of President John Tyler's proposed annexation of Texas is unsurprising: He "did not believe in enlarging our field, but in keeping our fences where they are and cultivating our present possession, making it a garden, improving the morals and education of our people."

Aside from delivering at least one good speech advocating volunteerism, Lincoln said nothing when Tyler's successor, James K. Polk, annexed Texas. When a border skirmish broke out over the land between the Rio Grande in the south and the Nueces River farther north, President Polk asked Congress for a declaration of war against Mexico. In April 1846, he got it.

Even after the commencement of hostilities with Mexico, Lincoln remained mute on the conflict there. In fact, in his campaign for Congress neither he nor his Democratic opponent mentioned the war.

Once Lincoln took his seat in the U.S. Congress, the majority of the fighting was over, and the Whigs were determined to make Polk's role in picking a fight to expand slave territory an issue in the coming campaign. In the House of Representatives, the Whigs' sole representative from Illinois, "the Lone Star of Illinois," as Lincoln had come to be called, spearheaded the attack on President Polk's prosecution of the war. His motives were mixed, and involved both altruistic impulses, such as being antislavery, and political concerns, such as his hope for rekindling the Whig Party's fortunes at the expense of the Democrats. In order to do this, Lincoln challenged Polk's motives for starting the war and, in turn, attempted to disrupt the financing of the coming occupation.

42 Lincoln's lodgings on the site of the Library of Congress

Congress convened in December 1847, over a year after Lincoln won his seat in the House. It took the Lincolns nearly five weeks to get to Washington, arriving there on December 2. After spending a brief amount of time in a local hotel, they moved into a boarding house run by Mrs. Anna G. Sprigg. Both of Lincoln's immediate predecessors, John J. Hardin and Edward D. Baker, had lived with Mrs. Sprigg during their terms in Congress, and Lincoln followed their example.

Lincoln spent the time before his departure for Washington in preparation for his extended absence. He leased his home in Springfield for $90 a year to a brick contractor named Cornelius Ludlum. He also made it clear in the lease that one of the upstairs bedrooms was reserved for storing the family's furniture. Obviously Lincoln did not intend his move to the nation's capital to be permanent.

Mrs. Sprigg's boarding house was close to the Capitol, standing on land now occupied by the Library of Congress. It was convenient for congressmen who did not maintain a residence in Washington (most didn't). What's more, the boarding house was partisan. All of the nine congressmen who lodged there were Whigs.

Lincoln was quite a hit with the other lodgers, employing his usual charm to win their friendship. At dinner, he defused sometimes tense political discussions (often about slavery) by telling funny story after funny story, usually leaving his messmates laughing. Lincoln also provided lively entertainment on frequent excursions to a neighborhood bowling alley. As a bowler, Lincoln apparently made up in enthusiasm what he lacked in skill. Dr. Samuel Busey, a fellow lodger at the Sprigg establishment, later recalled that Lincoln was "a very awkward bowler," and that he "played the game with great zest and spirit, solely for exercise and amusement." Of course, being Lincoln, he was also always quick with a joke or a ribald quip. As Dr. Busey put it, many of Lincoln's stories "were pretty broad."

At first, Washington, D.C., seemed a wonder to both Abraham Lincoln and his wife, Mary. It was far and away the largest city in which either of them had ever resided. Because they were a transient congressional family, the doors of Washington's high society were closed to the Lincolns, but there were biweekly Marine Band concerts on the grounds of the executive mansion and other diversions to be had. They regularly attended levees at the Polk White House— dull affairs, because the Polks refused to serve refreshments.

Because her husband worked long hours in his congressional office and spent his free time socializing with the other lodgers and friends he made in the federal government, Mary Todd Lincoln quickly tired of Washington. After all, if she had wanted to be cooped up all day by herself with only her small children, she could have done it just as well back home in Springfield or on her father's plantation in Lexington, Kentucky. In the spring of 1848, Mary Todd Lincoln opted for the latter, taking her children with her on a trip to visit her father in Kentucky. For his part, Lincoln barely missed her at first. His wife's absence gave him more time to apply himself to the task of representing his district. In his own words, when Mary was still there in D.C. with him, she "hindered me some in attending to business."

 ## 43 Congressional "spot resolutions"

In his war message to Congress in 1846, President James K. Polk claimed that Mexican troops had "shed American blood on American soil." As part of the Whig opposition's challenge to the legitimacy of Polk's reasoning for declaring war on Mexico, freshman congressman Abraham Lincoln responded by introducing a number of resolutions before the U.S. House of Representatives. He requested that the president make available to the people of the United States "all the facts which go to establish whether the particular spot of soil on which the blood of our citizens was so shed, was, or was not, our own soil."

Lincoln worked assiduously to polish these "spot resolutions" before introducing them because he had high hopes they would draw attention to him and the Whig cause. They did neither. Largely ignored by both the Whig and Democratic press when Lincoln introduced them, they were all but forgotten for most of a decade, until Lincoln's emergence as a leader of the Republican Party in the late 1850s.

Part of the problem was that he was a little late. Congress had declared war in April of 1846. Lincoln wasn't even elected to Congress until November of that year, and because of electoral rules then in place he did not take his seat until December of the following year.

Lincoln introduced his initial "spot resolution" during his first month in office, on December 22, 1847. This was nearly two years after Polk's war message, after the majority of the fighting was over. By this time General Zachary Taylor's troops in northern Mexico had won a decisive victory at Buena Vista, and General Winfield Scott had taken his forces ashore at Vera Cruz, following in the footsteps of Cortés, right to the "halls of Montezuma," Mexico City itself.

The Whigs' attack on Polk's war conduct had little to do with actual dissent over what Polk had wanted so badly. Rather, it was politically motivated. With 1848 an election year, the Whigs hoped to make hay out of Polk's use of dubious intelligence to mislead the American people into a war of expansion by claiming that the war was one of necessity.

This was not to say that there was not genuine disagreement among the Whigs over the war itself. The war was generally unpopular in the North, especially in New England. Residents of border states such as Illinois generally supported the war and showed patriotism across party lines. Lincoln's predecessors (John J. Hardin and Edward D. Baker, both Whigs) representing the Illinois Seventh District volunteered for service in the war. Baker was wounded at Cerro Gordo, and Hardin was killed at Buena Vista.

For all that, Lincoln gave several terrific speeches on the subject. In January of 1848, he called on the president to answer the questions he had posed in his previous speech: "Let him answer, fully, fairly, and candidly. Let him answer with *facts*, and not with arguments." If Polk could do so, Lincoln said, he would side with the president on this issue. Moving from a tight scrutiny of the facts to a broader speculation on Polk's motives, Lincoln posited that the president had started the war because of a hunger for "military glory—that attractive rainbow, that arises in showers of blood—that serpent's eye, that charms to destroy."

Lincoln had high hopes that the rhetoric in this speech would bring him attention in Washington and at home, thereby announcing his arrival on the national political scene. He was disappointed.

The House of Representatives did not debate his resolutions, nor did it adopt them. The president, a prolific diarist and letter writer, never mentioned Lincoln in either his correspondence or his diary. And although Whig papers such as the *Baltimore Patriot* and the *Missouri Republican* praised Lincoln's resolutions, the national print media made no reference to either Lincoln or his resolutions. Lincoln naturally received critical attention from Democratic papers back home in Illinois.

To make matters worse, many of Lincoln's political allies in Illinois strongly differed with him in his newly stated position on the war. His law partner William H. Herndon mentioned that "murmurs of dissatisfaction began to run through the Whig ranks," and old friends like Dr. Anson G. Henry glumly speculated that if the Whigs insisted on taking and holding this antiwar stance, along with insisting that the United States not annex any territory as a result of winning the war with Mexico, they would be out of power "for a very long time."

So the short-term outcome of Lincoln's hard work and political gambling could not have been further from the one he hoped for when he proposed the first of these resolutions in December 1847. His political enemies in the press either tarred him as a traitor or ignored him altogether, as did the majority of his political friends. Official Washington ignored him, and his resolutions died without even being debated.

44 Lincoln's career as a U.S. congressman

In 1846, Abraham Lincoln won a seat representing the Seventh Illinois Congressional District in the U.S. House of Representatives. You would think our (arguably) greatest president might have given his peers in the government (and by association, the country) a hint of the future during his initial foray into federal government service.

The answer is no. Lincoln had agreed to serve only one term and not run for re-election, as was then the custom in the Whig Party. Lincoln made a point of being present in his assigned committee meetings. During the two years he spent in Congress, he missed only thirteen out of 456 roll call votes.

Since he had no secretarial staff of his own, Lincoln answered all of his own official correspondence, often working late into the night at his boarding house. Like every other congressman of his time, Lincoln did his best to procure federal positions for party office-seekers from his district. Of course, since he was a freshman Whig congressman serving in a Democratic presidential administration, the deck was pretty much stacked against him.

Some have called the U.S. House of Representatives in the nineteenth century a repository of mediocrity. Lincoln's term in the House demonstrates how sometimes mediocrity is more a result of a lack of opportunity than a lack of ability.

45 Campaign work for Zachary Taylor

Lincoln had his greatest lasting impact as a U.S. congressman in his efforts to ensure a Whig victory in the 1848 presidential election. Whig leadership felt the Democrats were vulnerable in the coming election, and that was why Lincoln, in a series of attacks coordinated with other House Whigs, had hammered away so relentlessly at the so-called spot resolutions (see number 43).

By early 1848, the bulk of the fighting in Mexico was over, a peace treaty was in the works, and the Whigs could take Polk to task without concern over whether their political actions might have an adverse effect on the troops in the field. A group of House Whigs including both Lincoln and Alexander H. Stevens of Georgia (future vice president of the Confederacy) thought they could deflect accusations of being disloyal because of their attacks on the president by nominating a career military man with success on the battlefield in the very war they were protesting.

Because he had never expressed an opinion on anything political, and thus would be difficult for the opposition to pin down on campaign issues, General Zachary Taylor seemed an obvious choice. "Old Rough and Ready" (as his troops called him) was a career army officer and hero of the battles of both Buena Vista and Resaca de la Palma. Lincoln agreed wholeheartedly with this choice. The question for him was not as much one of ability as of electibility. "I am in favor of General Taylor," he said, "because I am satisfied we can elect him, that he would give us a Whig administration, and that we can not elect any other Whig."

Although Lincoln was a longtime admirer of Whig Party founder and leader Henry Clay, he questioned whether Clay could get elected. He said, "I go for [Taylor] not because I think he would make a better president than Clay, but because I think he would make a better one than Polk, or [Senator Lewis] Cass, or [Secretary of State James] Buchanan, or any such creatures, one of whom is sure to be elected if he is not."

Lincoln proved as good as his words, working tirelessly first for Taylor's nomination, then for his campaign once the general had been persuaded to accept the Whig nomination. He attended the Whig National Convention in Philadelphia as a Taylor delegate as well.

For Lincoln and the other young members of the Whig delegation to the House, getting Taylor elected was only the beginning. Lincoln understood that the Whig Party needed to reform itself if it wished to capture the hearts and minds of American voters, since many of its positions on issues of national importance seemed outdated and hide-bound.

In 1848 Whig Party stalwarts were not getting any younger—Henry Clay was seventy-one, and Daniel Webster was sixty-six and in ill health. If the party was going to remain a viable national entity, it needed vigorous new leadership.

Lincoln and his allies had few illusions that Zachary Taylor himself could spearhead party reform. Rather, they hoped to surround Taylor with potential new Whig leaders who could use their positions of power to begin the transformation process.

And so Lincoln campaigned vigorously for Zachary Taylor in 1848. He gave a stump speech on the floor of the House, using his keen wit to poke fun at both the Democratic Party and Democratic presidential candidates such as Lewis Cass. (James K. Polk did not bother to run for re-election, citing health issues. He died within a year of leaving the White House.) A Whig newspaper said that while giving this speech Lincoln "was so good-natured, and his style so peculiar, that he kept the House in a continuous roar of merriment for the last half hour."

When Congress recessed in mid-August, Lincoln remained in the nation's capital to continue working for the campaign. He helped edit the Whig campaign's official newspaper; he wrote countless letters on behalf of the Whig Executive Committee of Congress; and he made the most of the national network of contacts he had begun to cultivate, sending out constant requests for campaign feedback from all corners of the country.

By summer's end Lincoln had embarked on a campaign trip for Taylor through New England, giving several speeches to local Whig assemblies. His oratorical style drew particular notice and comment. Rather than observing the custom of the day, and standing formally behind a lectern for hours on end, Lincoln would commence his speech "leaning himself up against a wall . . . and talking in the plainest manner, and in the most indifferent tone, yet gradually fixing his footing, and getting command of his limbs, loosening his tongue, and firing up his thoughts, until he had got entire possession of himself and of his audience."

After several weeks in New England and New York, Lincoln returned to Illinois for the rest of the congressional recess. He had done his bit for Taylor and was optimistic about Taylor's chances in the coming election. In fact, the election of 1848 was a last flash of glory before the Whig candle winked out, a casualty of increasing sectional conflict over domestic issues during the 1850s. In November 1848, Zachary Taylor became the last Whig president elected to office.

46 What did Lincoln think about term limits?

Like most people, Lincoln's attitude on term limits was not static. When it benefited him politically he favored limiting the amount of time a politician could serve in any one post.

For example, when Lincoln was interested in running for Congress, but couldn't quite muster the support to get him the Whig Party nomination over such allies, and sometime rivals, as John J. Hardin and Edward D. Baker, the Whig Party's support of term limits benefited him. When he himself was called upon to honor that same Whig Party plank, he did so, albeit reluctantly.

Although term limits, as we understand the phrase today, did not exist in the nineteenth century, the idea behind them was alive and well. From the colonial era onward Americans were concerned over power concentrating into the hands of the wealthy, who might use political influence to further enrich themselves.

During the nineteenth century, it was a political maxim that George Washington's precedent as the national government's first chief executive should be followed by every president who succeeded him. In other words, the fact that Washington served two terms and no more as president bound those who followed him into the executive mansion. But while the tradition was consistent within the presidency, it varied in the House and Senate. Career politicians such as Henry Clay, Daniel Webster, and John C. Calhoun began their careers with multiple terms in the House, served in the executive branch (each of them spent at least one term as secretary of state, and Calhoun was vice president for nearly a decade), and eventually moved to the Senate.

Interestingly (or perhaps ironically) enough, it was the party of Clay and Webster that began to push the idea of limiting their members' terms in the House. Although there was no law on the books that required a candidate for the House to limit himself to one term, many of the Whig Party machines at the state level insisted that candidates voluntarily agree to limit themselves to a single term in the House. Unlike many politicians today, backtracking on that sort of promise in the 1840s would have been political suicide.

So when John J. Hardin won the Whig Party nomination for the Illinois Seventh Congressional District in 1842, he obligated himself to a single term, and all but assured that one of his opponents (Edward D. Baker) would succeed him as the Whig nominee in the district during the next election in 1844. Baker also knew that Lincoln was "in line" behind him after he served the term to which he was elected in 1844.

Obviously Lincoln was pleased by the opportunities this system of political patronage afforded when he was on the outside looking in. Once elected and serving in the Thirtieth Congress, he found that the life of a sitting politician in high national office appealed to him. Although he was well aware that he was bound by the promise he'd made to run for only one term in Congress, he did hint that he was willing to serve more than one term consecutively. When his law partner William H. Herndon mentioned to Lincoln that he had heard talk of his possible re-election, Lincoln pointed out his promise to serve only one term. But, in an interesting nod to the seductiveness of power, he added, "If it should so happen that nobody else wishes to be elected, I could not refuse the people the right of sending me again."

47 Refusing governorship of the Oregon Territory

In 1849, Abraham Lincoln was a lame-duck congressman wondering where his twin careers in public life and private law practice would take him next. He had campaigned hard for incoming President Zachary Taylor, and could have reasonably expected to receive an appointment to at least a middle-level office in the Taylor administration.

But he didn't actively seek a position until he discovered that the biggest plum job to be filled by an Illinois Whig was about to go to Justin Butterfield, a Chicago lawyer and former U.S. attorney for Illinois during the Harrison and Tyler administrations.

Butterfield was up for the position of commissioner of the General Land Office, which was a powerful one. It carried with it the ability to name one's own staff (yet another form of patronage), and the then-fat salary of $3,000 per year. Lincoln had no problem with Butterfield personally. Butterfield, he said, "is my personal friend, and is qualified to do the duties of the office." The problem was that Butterfield had supported Henry Clay in the Whig nomination process of 1848. Even after General Zachary Taylor's nomination for president, Butterfield had been lukewarm on Taylor's candidacy, doing nothing to support it, and certainly not campaigning for Taylor himself.

As Lincoln put it: "Of the quite one hundred Illinoisians, equally well qualified, I do not know one with less claims to (the position of commissioner of the General Land Office)." He didn't stop there, though. He called the potential commissioning of Butterfield "an egregious political blunder," then put his own name up for consideration.

After a furious letter-writing campaign attempting to drum up support for his candidacy, Lincoln traveled from Springfield back to Washington, D.C., where both he and Butterfield pled their respective cases before Interior Secretary Thomas Ewing. Butterfield had the inside track from the outset, producing recommendations from such prestigious Whigs as Henry Clay and Daniel Webster. He also had a letter signed by Whigs from Lincoln's home district in central Illinois claiming to be unhappy with Lincoln's service in the U.S. House of Representatives.

When Ewing awarded the job to Butterfield, it cemented Lincoln's dissatisfaction with the new administration. In Lincoln's opinion, Taylor and his staff should have been using the patronage at their disposal to help shore up the Whig Party's sagging unity, rather than playing the usual game of rewarding cronies.

Interestingly enough, Secretary of State John M. Clayton offered Lincoln a position as secretary to the governor of the Oregon Territory. This was quite a backhanded compliment to a former House member and an indefatigable campaigner for the new administration. Lincoln immediately refused the offer. Ewing realized that his cabinet colleague had unintentionally snubbed a hardworking and loyal Whig Party man from a state where they could muster few such party members, and promptly offered Lincoln the governorship of the Oregon Territory.

Lincoln considered it briefly, then rejected that offer as well because Oregon was a Democratic bastion, and a Whig like Lincoln could never expect to be elected to national office from there. Also, his second son, Edward, suffered from chronic poor health, and a move to the West Coast might cause him to take a turn for the worse. Lincoln cited his wife's disapproval as his reason for declining the offer, but in truth, he'd had quite enough of politics for the moment.

The indecision and misdirection of the Whig Party, the disarray of its aging national leadership, and its inability to codify a set of bedrock principles for which it stood, all served to sour Lincoln on his chances for advancement within its ranks. Besides, money was short, and he needed to tend to his law practice. So Abraham Lincoln retired from public life, probably little realizing how brief that retirement would be.

48 Temporary political retirement: Work as a successful trial lawyer

When Abraham Lincoln returned to Springfield at the end of his congressional career in 1849, he had his work cut out for him. His law practice, neglected during two years away in Washington, D.C., had suffered considerably. Although his partner William H. Herndon had stayed in Springfield to tend to firm business, Lincoln was the one who got them top dollar for their work. He was possibly the best trial lawyer in the state of Illinois. Herndon, on the other hand, was better at managing day-to-day business, which was not saying much. Lincoln was terribly unorganized!

Lincoln and Herndon made a superb team. Herndon did the research and Lincoln argued the cases. This arrangement played to both their strengths: Lincoln was, after all, affable, folksy, likable, shrewd, and able to lead a jury where he most wanted them to go without making it obvious. For his part, Herndon was a first-rate digger, and his exhaustive research left Lincoln amply prepared once they went to trial.

Soon after Lincoln's return to Springfield in 1849, he was admitted to practice before the United States Supreme Court. When Lincoln argued a case before the Supreme Court that same year it was a serious boost to his professional prestige. He also made headway arguing cases before the Illinois State Supreme Court.

At first the majority of Lincoln's legal work came from representing companies headquartered outside of Illinois, usually in attempts to resolve debts state residents owed them. Lincoln hated this tedious, expensive, and time-consuming work. Once he began to get enough work from other areas of practice, he resolved to quit hunting down and suing debtors for companies such as the St. Louis–based wholesale firm of Samuel C. Davis & Company. When he severed his relationship with them, he laid out very clearly why he was no longer doing the sort of work they required: "My mind is made up. I will have no more to do with this class of business. I can do business in Court, but I can not, and will not follow executions all over the world."

And "business" is precisely what Lincoln was doing. According to Sangamon County Circuit Court records, the firm of Lincoln & Herndon was involved in almost one-fifth of the cases argued before it. By 1853 that number had jumped to approximately one-third.

Among the reasons for this spike in Lincoln's cases was his reputation for both honesty and shrewdness. In an 1850 speech regarding the nature of the law, Lincoln said, "Let no young man, choosing the law for a calling, for a moment yield to this popular belief [that lawyers are dishonest]. Resolve to be honest at all events; and if, in your own judgment, you cannot be an honest lawyer, resolve to be honest with being a lawyer. Choose some other occupation."

Lincoln was also a killer in the courtroom: a genuine master of the rare art of handling juries, he could close a case like a freight train. Leonard Swett, a lawyer from nearby Bloomington, who knew Lincoln from his circuit court travels, noted Lincoln's conversational style, and the methodical manner in which he dealt with witnesses and made his summations. "Any man who took Lincoln for a simple-minded man," Swett once said, "would very soon wake up with his back in a ditch."

After watching Lincoln's closing arguments in a particular case, a reporter wrote of him, "Though he may have his equal, it would be no easy task to find his superior." What's more, Lincoln was inexpensive. He made a point of charging nominal fees in an age when nominal meant small. He rarely charged more than $10 or $20, and he firmly believed that clients should never be overcharged. In fact, when a client paid him $25 on what Lincoln considered a $15 fee, he returned $10, writing to his client: "You must think I am a high-priced man. You are too liberal with your money. Fifteen dollars is enough for the job."

Eventually, Lincoln's practice began to center around questions arising from railroad law. Railroads proliferated rapidly in the 1850s, especially in Lincoln's home state of Illinois. As a longtime supporter of internal transportation improvement, Lincoln enthusiastically involved himself in litigation that inevitably followed in the wake of rail expansion.

Working as a railroad attorney was lucrative for Lincoln. It also afforded him the opportunity to make new law. He argued so persuasively in favor of certain positions that rulings in his favor entered case law as precedent. In the first such case he argued, where he represented the Alton & Sangamon Railroad against an obstinate stockholder who refused to pay his share of the company's startup stock because of a change to the railroad's proposed route, Lincoln won a convincing and influential victory. In 1851 Lincoln represented the Illinois Central Railroad for the first time. This client would make frequent use of his services over the rest of the decade. In this case, *Illinois Central Railroad v. The County of McLean*, Lincoln's brilliant and reasoned argument against the right of municipalities to tax a railroad that the state itself had chartered as a tax-exempt enterprise saved his clients more than $500,000 in taxes per year.

Ironically, Lincoln had to sue the Illinois Central in order to collect the $5,000 fee he charged them once the case was decided in 1856. However, he was such a good lawyer that the railroad used him again and again throughout the 1850s, up until he ran for the presidency in 1860. If that isn't a testament to Lincoln's success as a trial lawyer and to the esteem in which his peers and the business community held for him, nothing is.

49 What invention did Lincoln register with the U.S. Patent Office?

For as much as he tried to distance himself from the tinkering father with whom he felt he had little in common, Abraham Lincoln was his father's son when it came to his fascination with things mechanical. According to Lincoln's law partner William H. Herndon, Lincoln "evinced a decided bent toward machinery or mechanical appliances, a trait he doubtless inherited from his father who was himself something of a mechanic and therefore skilled in the use of tools."

Lincoln, who had been a riverboat man in his youth, believed that riverboats, railroads, and transportation improvements were the keys to unlocking America's economic potential, so he made a point of staying abreast of them. In 1849, he wedded these twin lifelong interests in an invention he submitted for approval by the U.S. Patent Office.

Even after leaving behind the notion of training to be a riverboat pilot, Lincoln never got riverboats out of his blood. He read widely on the subject of river navigation, and when he came home from serving in Congress in 1849, he began to work on an idea to improve river transportation.

Lincoln's idea involved shoals and getting steamers over them. The device he invented used what he called adjustable buoyant chambers. He got the idea when, returning home to Illinois during a congressional recess, the riverboat he was traveling on ran aground on a shoal, and the captain had his crew use empty airtight casks to help refloat it.

According to Herndon, "Lincoln had watched this operation very intently . . . Continual thinking on the subject of lifting vessels over sand bars and other obstructions in the water suggested to him the idea of inventing an apparatus for this purpose." During what little spare time he had once Congress had reconvened, Lincoln began to draft ideas for a machine that improved upon and streamlined the process he'd witnessed.

Shortly after the expiration of his congressional term in 1849, Lincoln completed his designs. A Springfield mechanic named Walter Davis helped Lincoln construct a model, and Herndon later remembered, "Occasionally [Lincoln] would bring the model in the office, and while whittling on it would descant on its merits and the revolution it was destined to work in steamboat navigation. Although I regarded the thing as impracticable I said nothing, probably out of respect for Lincoln's reputation as a boatman."

Soon afterward, in 1849, Lincoln submitted his plans to the U.S. Patent Office for approval of a patent. As part of the application process, Lincoln wrote:

Be it known that I, Abraham Lincoln, of Springfield, in the county of Sangamon, in the state of Illinois, have invented a new and improved manner of combining adjustable buoyant air chambers with a steam boat or other vessel for the purpose of enabling their draught of water to be readily lessened to enable them to pass over bars, or through shallow water, without discharging their cargoes.

That same year the Patent Office awarded Lincoln his patent. Later, Herndon wryly commented "the invention was never applied to any vessel, so far as I ever learned, and the threatened revolution in steamboat architecture and navigation never came to pass."

Herndon's sarcasm notwithstanding, Lincoln's patent award was a singular achievement. Also, it is a valuable window into the workings of the mind of one of the most remarkable men ever to occupy the White House. Abraham Lincoln remains the only president of the United States to be awarded a patent. Not even a polymath like Thomas Jefferson can claim that honor.

50 The "chicken-bone case"

Much has been made of Abraham Lincoln's ability in the courtroom. A self-educated, slow-talking product of the frontier himself, Lincoln was able to connect with juries across the Illinois frontier and use his keen instinctual grasp of group psychology to get what he wanted out of them. Nowhere was this more apparent than in Lincoln's conduct of *Fleming* v. *Rodgers & Crothers*, the so-called chicken-bone case.

The case arose from the conduct of two Illinois doctors treating a man who had both legs broken when a chimney collapsed on him. Samuel G. Fleming lived in Bloomington, Illinois, where he worked as a carpenter. In the early-morning hours of October 17, 1855, a fire broke out, burning several large buildings in Bloomington. The chimney of one these buildings collapsed on top of the unfortunate Fleming, breaking bones in both of his thighs. Drs. Eli K. Crothers, Thomas P. Rogers, and Jacob R. Freese treated him.

For two weeks the patient seemed to be healing well. After sixteen days Fleming complained of severe pain along the fracture line in his right thigh. His sister, who was tending to him, said that she could feel in his leg where the break had not been set properly. Rogers was out of town, so Crothers re-examined the leg, concluded that it was properly set, and upped Fleming's morphine dosage. When the pain did not abate, Crothers looked at the leg again and declared Fleming's pain the result of having pleurisy.

Rogers returned to town twenty-four days after the fire, visited Fleming, and removed his dressing. Fleming's sister claimed that upon seeing Fleming's legs, Rogers said they "were crooked as ram's horns." He called in Crothers and Freese and they (rather tardily) reversed the previous diagnosis, noting that Fleming's right leg was now close to one inch shorter than his left.

More than a week later, the three doctors concluded that the bone had not set properly, and would need to be rebroken and then reset. At first Fleming agreed, but after chloroform was administered, Fleming changed his mind and begged them to stop. Crothers explained that if they didn't rebreak and reset the leg, Fleming might have a limp, and suffer from continual pain. Fleming replied that he wanted them to "let him alone, he had suffered enough." They redressed the leg and allowed it to heal with a crooked set.

Later, Fleming brought suit against Rogers and Crothers, and they hired Lincoln as one of their counsels. Once court proceedings began, Lincoln acted as lead counsel for the defense.

Initially the case looked pretty bad for Lincoln's clients. They had clearly botched the initial setting (not an altogether uncommon occurrence, in an age with no x-ray equipment, and in light of the swelling from Fleming's initial injury), and Crothers had made matters worse by doing a bad job on his second examination of Fleming's leg.

Here was where Lincoln's ability to lead frontier juries came into play. Lincoln set about making a study of basic bone structure after several lengthy continuances, and asked Dr. Crothers himself for assistance. Crothers used chicken bones to show Lincoln how bones grow and lose their flexibility and vitality as a body ages. Lincoln knew that when dealing with a frontier jury, points of law mattered little. The simpler he could make the argument, the more telling the visual, the better it would play.

Once in court, Lincoln saved the chicken-bone display for his summation. Holding up one bone from an older chicken, he snapped it in two, showing how easily it broke. Then he used the bone from a younger chicken and showed how much more flexible it was. According to Crothers's daughter Lulu, who later wrote about Lincoln's courtroom performance, Lincoln could not "remember about the lime or calcium deposited in older people's bones," so he held up the bone of the older chicken again, and talked about how an older bone "has the starch all taken out of it."

Lincoln's summation had better results than he could have reasonably hoped for based on the merits of the case. A jury that had likely been leaning toward finding for the plaintiff wound up hung, unable to agree on a verdict. The plaintiff and the defendants eventually settled out of court, and the case was never retried.

 **The Compromise of 1850**

In 1850, "the Great Compromiser," seventy-three-year-old Henry Clay, pulled off the last political deal of his distinguished career. Clay, perennial Whig candidate for president, former Speaker of the House of Representatives, former secretary of state, and longtime member of the U.S. Senate, was the architect of the Missouri Compromise, which had eased sectional tensions over the question of slavery thirty years before. By the time his last compromise fell apart under increasing sectional pressure four years later, Clay was dead. He had succeeded in averting a civil war at least twice in his lifetime.

The compromise itself came about as a result of questions such as: Should the newly populous state of California enter the Union as a "free" or a "slave" state? What about the rest of the territory wrested from Mexico? Should Texas be allowed to set the Rio Grande as not only its southern, but its western border as well? Should slavery be abolished in the District of Columbia? Should the South be awarded a federal law compelling Northern law enforcement entities to assist Southern sheriffs in apprehending runaway slaves?

Because neither side could muster the votes to prevail in Congress, Clay stepped forward with his compromise package in January 1850. Clay was in an uncomfortable spot. Although he represented Kentucky, a slave state, Clay was interested in phasing slavery out, and in favor of the so-called colonization movement, which called for African-Americans, both slave and free, to be shipped (voluntarily) to the African country of Liberia.

Clay proposed splitting the issues down the middle. Because California had passed a "free state" constitution the previous year, California was to be admitted to the Union as a free state. Further, the slave trade in Washington, D.C., was abolished (although slavery itself was to remain legal). These were both concessions to such congressional Northern antislavery extremists as William H. Seward of New York and Salmon P. Chase of Ohio.

Texas eventually lost its claim to most of its northwestern frontiers (now parts of Colorado, New Mexico, and Nebraska). In compensation for these lost territories, the U.S. Congress voted to award Texas $10,000,000. This question of whether to allow Texas to keep all of the territory it claimed, then whether or not to compensate the Lone Star State for the "loss" of far western border territories its citizens had not even occupied, had been the major sticking point in the Compromise of 1850. As such, the issue required its own sort of "sub-compromise," in order to get the rest of the original compromise passed through Congress.

In return for agreeing to the other parts of Clay's compromise, the South received the Federal Fugitive Slave Law, along with the assurance that slavery would be accepted and protected in the New Mexico Territory (which then included Arizona and part of Nevada). In truth, these assurances were losing propositions. Slavery was only viable in sections of the country where labor-intensive cash crops like cotton were grown. The climates of New Mexico and Arizona were not conducive to growing cotton, so slavery never developed roots there. As for the Fugitive Slave Law, it was rarely enforced in the North. If anything, it served as a constant reminder to Northerners of decades of Southern domination of the U.S. Senate.

For his part, Lincoln never clearly expressed an opinion on one side or the other. He did later note that the Compromise of 1850 permanently split the moribund Whig Party. After 1850 it was not enough to be a Whig. You were either a "Conscience Whig" (and hence, antislavery) or a "Cotton Whig" (pro-slavery). Lincoln commented in the mid-1850s that he was "always a Whig," but by the time he said it, the Whig Party was already dead, if not yet buried.

The Compromise of 1850 helped to place the discussion of slavery and what to do about it in the forefront of the American political scene. Politicians such as Lincoln, who were nominally antislavery without being outright abolition-ists, found themselves unable to avoid deeper consideration of the subject of slavery, as they once had. At this point, Abraham Lincoln's views on the insti-tution of slavery began to undergo a profound transformation. Nowhere was this more apparent than in his remarks at the end of a eulogy delivered on the occasion of Henry Clay's death, in 1852. Clay, Lincoln said, "did not perceive, that on a question of human right, the Negroes were to be excepted from the human race." Unfortunately, Clay's compromise did little to save the party he'd helped found, and nothing to abate the suffering of those already in bondage. All it really did was delay a conflict that both Northerners and Southerners were coming to see as inevitable.

52 Was Lincoln an abolitionist or not?

This is a ticklish question because, like most people, Lincoln's opinions gradually changed over the course of his life. While he was emphatically and consistently antislavery his entire life, he was not, at first, an abolitionist. Like many other Northerners, Lincoln was put off by the extremism and stridency of hardcore abolitionists. (A contemporary parallel would be how most people, regardless of how they feel about abortion, look on those who are extremists on either side of the current pro-life/pro-choice debate). However, eventually the slavery debate forced Lincoln to choose.

Lincoln imbibed antislavery sentiments at an early age from his father, Thomas. Thomas Lincoln hated slavery in large part because, as an uneducated free white laborer growing to manhood in western Kentucky (where slavery was legal), he had to compete for his livelihood with cheaper black slave labor. Understandably, he resented it.

For his own part, Abraham Lincoln frequently referred to himself as "naturally antislavery." Early in his political career, Lincoln illustrated his seemingly contradictory position in a written protest he co-submitted to the Illinois State Legislature with a colleague named Daniel Stone. The two wrote that "the institution of slavery is founded on both injustice and bad policy." At that time, however, Lincoln wasn't interested in actively or officially discouraging slavery because, he believed "the Congress of the United States has no power, under the Constitution, to interfere with the institution of slavery in the different states."

What's more, as a practicing trial lawyer, Lincoln further muddied his record on slavery regulation by representing people on either side of the issue in open court. Bear in mind that Lincoln's job description as a lawyer included arguing on behalf of clients with whom he did not necessarily agree personally.

In 1841 he argued against the classification as slave of a young black woman named Nance whose owner was trying to sell her in Tazewell County. The Illinois Supreme Court agreed with him in this particular case (*Bailey* v. *Cromwell*), saying, "The presumption of law was, in this State, that every person was free, without regard to color. . . . The sale of a free person is illegal."

However, Lincoln took on another client in 1847, a wealthy Kentuckian named Matson. Matson was suing to retrieve slaves who had run away when he brought them from his plantation in Kentucky to work on land he owned in southern Illinois. In arguing this case, Lincoln claimed that Matson was entitled to the right of transit. According to Lincoln, it was true that the Northwest Ordinance of 1787 forbade slavery in the Old Northwest Territory (which included all land north of the Ohio and east of the Mississippi and, hence, the entire state of Illinois). But since Matson was bringing his slaves into Illinois to work his land there for a fixed amount of time, he had a reasonable expectation that his property rights would be respected. The court didn't buy Lincoln's argument, and to make matters worse, Matson stiffed him on his fee.

Moderate Northerners (including Lincoln) took the position that fencing in slavery where it already existed and not overly antagonizing Southerners was the best way to deal with the issue. Slavery would cease to be viable, they theorized, if it were not allowed to expand territorially. All of this came to a head over Texas, during the annexation debates. "Individually I never was much interested in the Texas question," Lincoln later recalled. "I never could see much good to come of annexation . . . on the other hand, I never could very clearly see how the annexation would augment the evil of slavery. It always seemed to me that slaves would be taken there in about equal numbers, with or without annexation."

As the nineteenth century moved into its second half, the middle ground on slavery's expansion began to erode. The Mexican War had brought vast new territories under American control, and proslavery leaders had plans to perpetuate slavery through this expansion. In response, the North endorsed the Wilmot Proviso, which called for the prohibition of slavery expansion into territory acquired as a result of the Mexican War. Lincoln did not publicly support this legislation, but he repeatedly voted for it while he was in the House of Representatives. In this social and political pressure cooker, with the two sides alarmingly polarized over the question of slavery, the issue became a political touchstone that smashed such national institutions as the Whig Party. The middle position became increasingly untenable.

Lincoln himself responded emotionally to Massachusetts senator Daniel Webster's ringing words during the debates over the Compromise of 1850: "Liberty *and* Union, one *and* indivisible!" Webster's speech echoed sentiments Lincoln had earlier expressed in a letter to an able young Whig protégé named Richard Yates. It was important not to advocate the containment of slavery at the expense of the Union, Lincoln said. If push came to shove, things like the

Wilmot Proviso would have to be jettisoned, because "of all political objects the preservation of the Union stands number one."

Lincoln repeated this maxim throughout his political career. Even as the furor over the Kansas-Nebraska Act of 1854 pulled him back into the political spotlight, even while he debated Senator Stephen A. Douglas over questions such as popular sovereignty, and even when he was nominated first for the Senate and then for the presidency by a new political party that was explicitly abolitionist, Lincoln never wavered. He publicly expressed an increasingly unpopular middle view: the Union first, above all things.

 ## 53 Lincoln's shifting views on abolitionism

Lincoln continued to put the Union above all else, even as his own personal views on slavery became more convicted. "If slavery isn't a sin," he said at one point, "nothing is." In 1855, Lincoln read *Sociology of the South*, an ill-disguised apologist piece by Virginian slavery advocate George Fitzhugh. Lincoln kept copious notes as he read Fitzhugh, commenting at one point, "Although volume upon volume is written to prove slavery a very good thing, we never hear of the man who wishes to take the good of it, by being a slave himself." Lincoln skewered Fitzhugh's central argument that slave labor was preferable to free labor when he wrote, "The most dumb and stupid slave that ever toiled for a master, does constantly know that he is wronged."

Later that same year, Lincoln despaired ever seeing a nonviolent resolution to the slavery issue, saying, "There is no peaceful extinction of slavery in prospect for us." Southerners were so intractable in their defense of slavery, and Northerners so entrenched in their growing antipathy for it, that the "condition of the negro slave in America . . . is now so fixed, and hopeless of change for the better, as that of the lost souls of the finally impenitent."

Yet, this was the able practitioner of politics as the "art of the possible." The same man who, as president of the United States at the height of the Civil War, wrote to firebrand abolitionist newspaper editor Horace Greeley:

If there be those who would not save the Union, unless they could at the same time save slavery, I do not agree with them. If there be those who would not save the Union unless they could at the same time destroy slavery, I do not agree with them. My paramount object in this struggle is to save the Union, and is not either to save or to destroy slavery. If I could save the Union without freeing any slave I would do it, and if I could save it by freeing all the slaves I would do it; and if I could save it by freeing some and leaving others alone I would also do that. What I do about slavery, and the colored race, I do because I believe it helps to save the Union; and what I forbear, I forbear because I do not believe it would help to save the Union. I shall do less whenever I shall believe what I am doing hurts the cause, and I shall do more whenever I shall believe doing more will help the cause. I shall try to correct errors when shown to be errors; and I shall adopt new views so fast as they shall appear to be true views. I have here stated my purpose according to my view of official duty; and I intend no modification of my oft-expressed personal wish that all men everywhere could be free.

Lincoln always maintained that he signed the Emancipation Proclamation as a political expedient, and not out of a personal sense of outrage over slavery. As Lincoln put it to one of his supporters in Springfield, Illinois, James Conkling, in late 1863: "You say you will not fight to free negroes. Some of them seem willing to fight for you; but, no matter. Fight you, then exclusively to save the Union. I issued the proclamation on purpose to aid you in saving the Union. Whenever you shall have conquered all resistance to the Union, if I shall urge you to continue fighting, it will be an apt time, then, for you to declare you will not fight to free negroes." And later in the same letter:

> *I thought that whatever negroes can be got to do as soldiers, leaves just so much less for white soldiers to do, in saving the Union. Does it appear otherwise to you? But negroes, like other people, act upon motives. Why should they do any thing for us, if we will do nothing for them? If they stake their lives for us, they must be prompted by the strongest motive—even the promise of freedom. And the promise being made, must be kept.*

So in the end, Abraham Lincoln *was* an abolitionist in action, if not in name. With the stroke of a pen, he abolished slavery in those areas of the United States that were still in rebellion against the federal government (or, as others have put it, "He freed no one"). In so doing, Lincoln set in motion the events that led to the ratification of the Thirteenth and Fourteenth amendments. He did it for the right reasons, but the politics of the time insisted that he deny his abolitionism. And yet he is known today as "the Great Emancipator." It is both as fitting and ironic a title as any given out over the course of American history.

54 Did Lincoln own slaves?

This question pops up in classrooms and on call-in talk-radio shows year-in, year-out. The short answer is no, Abraham Lincoln never, ever owned slaves. Interestingly enough, the long answer isn't really all that long, either, and it's just as definitive as the short answer.

In some ways, it is unsurprising that this question arises. On the face of it, Lincoln had all the makings of a doughface, a Northern man with Southern sympathies. "I must confess I am afraid of 'Abe,'" an abolitionist acquaintance wrote during Lincoln's unsuccessful quest for the U.S. Senate in 1854. "He is Southern by birth, Southern in his associations, and Southern, if I mistake not, in his sympathies. . . . His wife, you know, is a Todd, of a pro-slavery family, and so are all his kin."

The author was technically correct in the above description, except for where Lincoln's sympathies lay. He was an out-and-out border-state man, and he did not like slavery. True, Lincoln's father-in-law, Robert Todd, was a Kentucky slaveholder, but he joined Henry Clay in trying to make slavery illegal. He worked to get the removal of the clause allowing slavery in the new Kentucky state constitution shortly before his death in 1849. He also ran for office as an antislavery, or a Conscience Whig.

As for Lincoln's "Southern" upbringing, he was born in Kentucky but into an antislavery household, with an uneducated laborer father who resented slave labor as cheap competition. As a result, Lincoln grew up antislavery (see number 52). What's more, no one in Lincoln's immediate family (mother, father, or sister) ever owned slaves.

His uncle Mordecai Lincoln, who had inherited the estate of Abraham's namesake grandfather upon his death, did own slaves, though, and Lincoln's wife, Mary, grew up on her father's Kentucky plantation with slaves to wait on her.

Lincoln also had a number of close friends who came from slaveholding backgrounds. Joshua Speed, a young storeowner with whom he shared a room when he first moved from New Salem to Springfield, Illinois, came from a wealthy Kentucky slaveholding family (and eventually went back to Kentucky to help run the family plantation).

As noted in number 53, Abraham Lincoln once said, "If slavery isn't a sin, then nothing is." These are hardly the words of a man who would entertain the idea of owning another human being.

55 How the Kansas-Nebraska Act brought Lincoln back into politics

Kansas-Nebraska really finished off Abraham Lincoln's political formation. His political principles had been case-hardened in fire and completely forged through by that point. Lincoln truly believed that "all men are created equal." Even though he did not believe that blacks were the intellectual equals of whites, he believed that in a republic they simply must be the political equals of whites. Radical stuff in 1854!

The Kansas-Nebraska Act was the brainchild of Illinois Democratic senator Stephen A. Douglas. As part of an attempt to solidify his own political base in the Democratic Party and answer the question of slavery's legal status once and for all, Douglas came up with legislation to deal with slavery in the federal territories that called for a repeal of the Missouri Compromise. (The Missouri Compromise had banned the extension of slavery into the territories more than thirty years before.)

Douglas did this partially to help speed the building of a transcontinental railroad through the previously unorganized Nebraska Territory. He could not get the railroad pushed through the Senate without Southern support, which included that of Missouri senator David Atcheson. Atcheson said he would gladly see Nebraska "sink in hell" before he allowed it to be organized as a free territory (which would follow the dictates of the Missouri Compromise). Also, without at least some Southern support, Douglas would never realize his dream of occupying the White House.

Douglas knew that any attempt to repeal the Missouri Compromise would cause "one hell of a storm." Thus, he was ready for a battle. What he wasn't prepared for was how his attempt to get the Kansas-Nebraska Act passed would unite antislavery forces in the North into a new opposition political party: the Republicans.

In Douglas's home state of Illinois, the man who became head of the Republican Party—Douglas's personal political nemesis—was none other than former Whig congressman and Illinois state legislator Abraham Lincoln. By 1854 Lincoln had been out of politics for nearly five years, and was instead focusing on his law practice. But Kansas-Nebraska galvanized Lincoln and drew him back into politics. Like many in the North who objected to slavery, Lincoln had been content to watch it be "fenced in" and contained where it existed, believing that if slavery were not allowed to expand, it would wither and die. When Southern politicians convinced Douglas to push for the repeal of the Missouri Compromise (which kept slavery out of the federal territories in the old Louisiana Purchase north of Missouri's southern border), Lincoln rose to oppose him.

Meeting Douglas on his own terms, Lincoln debated Douglas's doctrine of popular sovereignty throughout 1854. (This doctrine allowed citizens of a soon-to-organize territory to decide for themselves whether they wanted to allow slavery.) Soon, Lincoln was the leading spokesman for a rough Illinois coalition of anti-Nebraska Democrats, nativists (opponents of foreign immigration), and antislavery Whigs, all of whom eventually gelled into the Republican Party. This party backed Lincoln for a U.S. Senate seat twice, and for the presidency in 1860.

56 The Senate election of 1854

The Kansas-Nebraska fight in 1854 touched off a chain of events that culminated in Abraham Lincoln's election as the sixteenth president of the United States six years later, in 1860. In the first place, Kansas-Nebraska finished destroying the already moribund Whig coalition. Freed of "Conscience Whig" versus "Cotton Whig" distinctions, the members of the old Whig Party were able to take part in the political realignment of the mid-1850s, which resulted in the Republican Party's birth. Drawing its membership from the ranks of radical abolitionists, Democrats who had broken with their former party over slavery expansion into the federal territories and Southern domination of that party, and conservative Whigs and nativists, known collectively as "Know Nothings," the new Republican Party was vigorously opposed to slavery expansion, if not to the actual practice of slavery where it already existed.

The Kansas-Nebraska Act repealed the Missouri Compromise and allowed for slavery in sections of the Louisiana Purchase where it had previously been prohibited. It also drew Abraham Lincoln out of political retirement and allowed him to exploit Kansas-Nebraska's weaknesses. In speech after speech, he attacked both the act and its principal sponsor, Senator Stephen A. Douglas, chairman of the Senate Committee on Territories. Douglas and Lincoln had been political rivals in Illinois state politics for close to two decades, and Lincoln simply could not resist the opportunity to challenge the far more successful Douglas one more time.

By the end of the Kansas-Nebraska fight, the electorate in many Northern states considered the Democratic Party too beholden to Southern special interests. They began to vote Democratic candidates out of office in their state and federal government delegations. This put anti-Nebraska forces in a position to elect the next U.S. senator from Illinois. (Douglas himself was not up for re-election again until 1858, but his protégé, and Lincoln's old dueling partner, James Shields, was up for re-election as a Democrat.)

These forces had yet to coalesce into the Republican Party, but Lincoln had come to prominence among all of them. He managed to offend none of them in the course of leading the fight against Kansas-Nebraska in Illinois that very year. His name began to make the rounds as the type of person anti-Nebraska legislators might want to send to the Senate.

Lincoln himself badly wanted to be elected to the U.S. Senate. He had buried his political ambition after his term in the U.S. House of Representatives had expired in 1849, but it had been rekindled through his war of words with Douglas over Kansas-Nebraska. His candidacy for the Senate was not without problems, though.

To gain support for Richard Yates's run for re-election to the U.S. House of Representatives, Lincoln had allowed himself to be placed on the ballot for his old seat in the Illinois State Legislature. However, he had been reluctant to do this for two reasons: First, no sitting member of the Illinois State Legislature could be elected to the Senate; second, having already served in the U.S. House of Representatives, returning to state-level government as anything other than a governor was a step backward for any politician.

To make matters worse, Yates lost his bid for re-election, while Lincoln himself won a seat in the legislature by the largest margin of any candidate for office in the state that year. Lincoln hemmed and hawed, and eventually refused the seat to which he had been elected. This left him free to run for the Senate, but open to charges that he ran for an office he had no intention of occupying.

Initially, Lincoln had a pretty good handle on the race for the Senate, with a large number of delegates pledged to him. However, as the voting continued, it became clear that he was losing delegates. He could either direct his supporters to vote for anti-Nebraska Democrat (and Lincoln's personal friend) the fiery Lyman Trumbull, or let the voting end with no clear candidate victorious. The Democrats hoped for the latter option, thinking that in a later session of the legislature they might be able to get Shield re-elected. Lincoln put party interests before personal interests (even though he really had no party, as the anti-Nebraska coalition had not yet formally merged into the Republican Party). He advised his supporters to vote for Trumbull. Once again, Lincoln had courted the national spotlight, only to be disappointed at the outcome.

However, if there was short-term disappointment, in the long-term, Lincoln benefited from how he ran his campaign and his public willingness to place his support in Trumbull's hands. The anti-Nebraska Democrats (mostly from southern Illinois) had been part of the block that had voted consistently against Lincoln. They were so impressed with how Lincoln conducted himself, they pledged themselves to supporting him against Stephen A. Douglas in the 1858 senatorial race. In addition to the old Whig allies Lincoln could still count on in central Illinois, the Chicago-based abolitionists also actively courted his participation. This cemented his chances of being the next Republican Senate nominee in Illinois.

57 The Dred Scott decision: The case that galvanized the Republican Party

If Kansas-Nebraska began to transition Lincoln and his political allies from old Whigs into new Republicans, the U.S. Supreme Court's decision in the *Scott v. Sanford* case finished the job. Dred Scott was the slave of an army surgeon named John Emerson, who took Scott from his birthplace in Missouri across the Mississippi to live with him while he was stationed at Rock Island, Illinois. But the Illinois state constitution expressly prohibited slavery within the state's borders, as did the Northwest Ordinance (which initially organized the Great Lakes states into one territory during the 1780s) before it. Next, Emerson took Scott with him to a posting at Fort Snelling in the Minnesota Territory, where the Missouri Compromise expressly prohibited slavery.

Probably because he didn't know that living for an extended period in free territory gave him standing to sue for his freedom, Scott did not bring suit against his owner until after Dr. Emerson died in 1843. At that point, Scott tried to buy his freedom from Emerson's widow. In 1847, Scott sued Emerson's brother-in-law John Sanford (because no woman, not even a widow, could hold property in America during the 1840s) for his freedom, claiming that living in Illinois and the Wisconsin Territory had given him status as a free man. Sanford was a resident of New York, and Scott attempted to get the case to federal court as quickly as possible by pointing out that the defendants, Mrs. Emerson and her brother, lived in different states.

For ten years the case played out both ways in the Missouri courts, until the U.S. Supreme Court agreed to hear the case in 1857. The issue before them was whether Scott, an African-American and a slave, had standing to bring suit at all.

In March 1857, just two days after Democrat James Buchanan's inauguration, the Court delivered its opinion. Actually, it delivered nine of them. Chief Justice Roger B. Taney insisted that rather than simply delivering a majority and a minority decision, all nine justices ought to write their own decisions.

Taney's own opinion spoke for the majority, though. In a sprawling, poorly argued, and inconsistent opinion, he wrote that Scott had no standing to bring suit in court because, as an African-American, he was ineligible to be a citizen, regardless of whether he was slave or free. According to Taney, neither the Declaration of Independence nor the U.S. Constitution said anything at all to establish blacks' rights to citizenship; therefore, Scott had no case. As Taney put it, blacks were "so far inferior, that they had no rights which the white man was bound to respect."

If the justices had ruled solely on the question of whether Scott was slave or free, public reaction might not have been as strong as it was. Because Taney was bent on delivering a definitive answer to the question of where slavery could and could not exist, he further ruled that living for a time in free territory did not entitle Scott to his freedom. The Constitution did not give Congress authority to limit slavery in any territories, and thus antislavery legislation such as the Missouri Compromise was "not warranted by the Constitution," so it was "therefore void."

Not surprisingly, this did not go over well in the North. Clergymen (the bedrock of the antislavery movement in the North) took to their pulpits and bitterly denounced Taney's decision. As a result, newspapers such as the *New York Herald* wrote that "the whole North will evidently be preached into rebellion against the highest constituted Court in the country." The die was cast and the Rubicon crossed. It was only a matter of time.

58 Distrust for the Supreme Court spurs Lincoln's abolitionism

For his part, Lincoln remained quiet on the Dred Scott ruling, at least at first. Lincoln had a lifelong and abiding respect for the rule of law, and he hesitated to criticize the highest court in the country. After reading Taney's opinion, Lincoln didn't see much cause for concern. He wrote later that he never "complained especially of the Dred Scott decision because it held a negro could not be a citizen," an opinion with which Lincoln agreed at the time. Although the Emancipation Proclamation and several of his wartime speeches offer tangible proof of how his opinion changed, that wasn't until later. However, where the Dred Scott decision affected Lincoln most tellingly was in changing his view of the Supreme Court and its role as final arbiter on federal legal matters, especially on the question of slavery. Previous to Dred Scott, Lincoln had said, "The Supreme Court of the United States is the tribunal to decide such questions."

Because of its sweeping nature, the Dred Scott decision caused Lincoln to note that if "this important decision had been made by the unanimous concurrence of the judges, and without any apparent partisan bias, and in accordance with legal public expectation, and with the steady practice of the departments throughout our history," then the American people ought to have quietly gone along with it. Of course, the ruling did no such thing, and Lincoln took particular issue with how Taney himself abused the "plain and unmistakable language of the Declaration [of Independence]" with his ridiculous assertion that the Founding Fathers never intended for the Declaration or the U.S. Constitution to apply to blacks. For Lincoln, that was enough. Taney's biased, partisan, and flawed ruling had permanently soured Lincoln on the idea that all Americans ought to view the word of the Supreme Court in general, and of the chief justice in particular, as the final authority. During his presidency Lincoln himself had occasion to put that maxim into practice, when he pointedly ignored Taney's ruling in *Ex Parte Merryman*, which called for Lincoln not to suspend the writ of habeas corpus (the right to a speedy trial).

For the time being, though, Taney's ruling had the immediate effect of pushing Abraham Lincoln more toward the abolitionist end of the political spectrum than he might have otherwise been comfortable with. And when senior U.S. senator Stephen A. Douglas appeared in Illinois in June 1857 to argue in defense of the ruling, Lincoln made his sentiments on the question known as he gave the Republican Party's rebuttal to Douglas. Lincoln called the Dred Scott decision "erroneous," saying the Republicans knew "the court that made it, has often over-ruled its own decisions, and we shall do what we can to have it to over-rule this. We offer no *resistance* to it." Then he ended his speech with a bang, framing the plight of African-Americans in an America where the rule of law insisted they abide by a code that forced compliance from them, yet did nothing to protect them:

All the powers of the earth seem rapidly combining against (the African American) . . . They have him in his prison house; they have searched his person, and left no prying instrument with him. One after another they have closed the heavy iron doors upon him, and now they have him, as it were, bolted in with a lock of a hundred keys, which can never be unlocked without the concurrence of every key; the keys in the hands of a hundred different men, and they scattered to a hundred different and distant places; and they stand musing as to what invention, in all the dominions of mind and matter, can be produced to make the impossibility of his escape more complete than it is.

Part 3

Lincoln and the U.S. Presidency

How did a successful lawyer from a frontier state, out of elective office for over a decade, manage to get himself elected president of the United States? What sorts of deals did Lincoln make with other Republican Party stalwarts? Was growing his beard merely a public relations move? Once he became president, what was life in the Lincoln White House like? What family tragedy overshadowed all of Lincoln's many accomplishments during this period? And is it true that Lincoln actually allowed a turkey to vote? Take a look . . .

59 What was Lincoln's best speech and why isn't there a transcript?

Is it the Gettysburg Address? No. The Second Inaugural? Nuh-uh. The "house divided" speech he gave during the 1858 Illinois senatorial race? Apparently not. According to none other than Lincoln's law partner William H. Herndon, Abraham Lincoln gave the speech of his life not at the dedication of the Gettysburg National Cemetery, not in Washington, D.C., on the occasion of his second inauguration as president, not during a senate race, but in Bloomington, Illinois, in 1856.

It went something like this: In 1856, the new Republican Party was still feeling its way around organizationally. As with any new organization, a bureaucracy needs to be set up and tasks must be identified and delegated. So from 1854 to 1856, the Republican Party sponsored a series of grass-roots-level organizational meetings to accomplish these sorts of goals.

One of these meetings took place on May 29, 1856, at Major's Hall (located on the third floor of the three-story building that housed Humphrey's Cheap Store) in Bloomington, Illinois. By this time, Herndon had acquired the habit of taking notes on his partner's speeches. Over forty reporters attended, and yet no complete record of the speech Lincoln gave to the delegates assembled there remains.

Lincoln's importance in the new Republican Party dictated that he give the last speech of the evening. By all accounts, it was a whopper. As Herndon later explained, he "attempted for about fifteen minutes, as was usual with me then to take notes, but at the end of that time I threw pen and paper away and lived only in the inspiration of the hour." Of all of the members of the press in attendance, only one, the correspondent sent by the *Alton Weekly Courier*, gave anything resembling a summary of Lincoln's address. According to the article the *Weekly Courier* later published, Lincoln laid out "the pressing reasons of the present moment," then went on to attack slavery as the root of the nation's many woes. In a break with his earlier position refusing to overtly target slavery or slaveholders, Lincoln condemned Southerners for attempting to paint slavery as not only positive in the lives of black slaves, but a potential solution to the problems suffered by many Northern laborers. (Lincoln probably mistook the writings of the proslavery firebrand George Fitzhugh as the consensus opinion of most Southerners on this point.)

From there, he went on to decry Illinois senator Stephen A. Douglas and the other Northern Democrats, claiming they too accepted the argument that slavery must be extended throughout the country. (He was wrong on this point. Douglas and the Northern wing of the party he led were trying to walk a razor's edge of compromise to forestall a split in the party's ranks, and they never did accept this argument.) According to Lincoln, the answer was for antislavery forces to put aside their differences. Conservative Whigs and anti-immigrant Know Nothings, Democrats who had broken with their former party over the question of the Kansas-Nebraska Act in 1854, radical abolitionists—they all needed to come together under the banner of the Republican Party to combat the encroachment of slavery into the North.

It was a rousing speech, and the ending was particularly effective. If Southerners responded to Northern attempts to halt slavery's encroachment by raising "the bugbear of disunion," Lincoln said, then the united opponents of slavery in the North must drive home forcefully to their countrymen in the South that "the Union must be preserved in the purity of its principles as well as in the integrity of its territorial parts." Lincoln would later echo this sentiment while retreating publicly from the notion that slavery was inconsistent with democratic principles by saying to Horace Greeley that as president his job was to preserve the Union, not to free the slaves. And yet before he was finished, he did both.

"His speech was full of fire and energy and force," Herndon later wrote. It "was logic; it was pathos; it was enthusiasm; it was justice, equity, truth, and right set ablaze by the divine fires of a soul maddened by the wrong; it was hard, heavy, knotty, gnarly, backed with wrath."

It was Abraham Lincoln.

60 How original was the "house divided" speech?

"A house divided against itself cannot stand.
I believe this government cannot endure, permanently
half *slave* and half *free*."

—Abraham Lincoln in his acceptance speech for the
Republican nomination to the U.S. Senate

The Gettysburg Address. The Second Inaugural. The Lincoln-Douglas debates. All great speeches given by a man immortalized as a speechmaker as no other in American history. Unlike many modern politicians, Abraham Lincoln wrote all of his own speeches. Also unlike modern politicians (and their speechwriters), Lincoln put a lot of thought into his speeches, perfecting them over weeks, months, even years. And he was not above recycling his best pieces if they would work in a later speech (something modern politicians might call "staying on message").

A perfect example of Lincoln's tendency to work things out slowly over and over when crafting his statements is the famous "house divided" speech. Lincoln gave it on the occasion of his nomination by the Republican Party for Senate in 1858, but his metaphor of the "house divided against itself" (which echoed the Bible, and would be familiar to his audience) dated back several years in his own writings.

The earliest example of Lincoln's use of this notion comes from his personal correspondence three years earlier. In 1855, Lincoln wrote, "Can we, as a nation, continue together *permanently—forever*—half slave, and half-free?" A year later, speaking in support of John C. Fremont's Republican presidential campaign, Lincoln stated on a number of different occasions "his opinion that our government could not last—part slave and part free." Yet another year later (in 1857), when Lincoln spoke out against the Southern-backed Lecompton Constitution designed to admit Kansas to the Union as a slave state, he used the phrase "a house divided against itself cannot stand."

So yes, Abraham Lincoln did, in fact, recycle the best portions of some of his speeches. It is interesting to note, though, that he did very little of this with such speeches as the Gettysburg Address and the Second Inaugural.

Lincoln v. Douglas:
61 The first debate and how it framed the conflict

In 1858, an adroit railroad lawyer with a solid reputation within his home state of Illinois challenged the emerging national leader of the Democratic Party for re-election to the United States Senate. Little-known outside of Illinois, Abraham Lincoln handily won the Republican Party's nomination for the Senate seat then occupied by "the Little Giant," Stephen A. Douglas.

In reality, the election was about far more than a Senate seat from Illinois. Abraham Lincoln insisted on making it a single-issue campaign on the question of slavery, and Douglas's amorphous and ambiguous position on it. The campaign, Lincoln said, was about "the difference between men who think slavery a wrong and those who do not think it a wrong."

According to the *New York Times*, the 1858 campaign season made Illinois "the most interesting political battleground in the Union." Lincoln challenged his longtime political nemesis Douglas to a series of seven debates, wherein Lincoln would put the national spotlight to good use, morphing himself from a political unknown into a nationally prominent political figure. Douglas would go on to win re-election in Illinois, and thus also win the battle. Two years later, though, Abraham Lincoln would go on to win the war.

The debates did not begin well for Lincoln. In remarks made at various times over the several months before the debates began in August of 1858, Lincoln referred to Douglas as something of a toothless lion. Douglas showed he had teeth in opening the first debate at Ottawa by launching a savage attack on Lincoln, claiming that Lincoln intended to enact a radical abolitionist agenda if elected senator.

Douglas caught Lincoln unprepared for such defamation. Lincoln's methodical temperament did not lend itself to the parry and thrust of active debate, and he stumbled through a lengthy and unfocused rebuttal of Douglas's claims that Lincoln intended to repeal the existing fugitive slave act, that Lincoln opposed the admission of more slave states into the Union, that Lincoln favored abolition of the slave trade in the District of Columbia, and so on. Although Lincoln afterward proclaimed himself satisfied with how things went for him in the first round, saying, "The fire flew some, and glad to know that I am yet alive," many of his closest supporters insisted that he lost ground at Ottawa. He needed to sharpen his responses to Douglas, take the offensive, and "put a few ugly questions" to the Little Giant.

62 Lincoln v. Douglas: Lincoln's response and the outcome of the debates

Lincoln struck back later when the two men met to debate at Freeport. He answered the questions Douglas had so damningly posed at Ottawa one by one. He was not associated with the radical ideas Douglas had mentioned in his own charges, Lincoln said, but he was "impliedly, if not expressly, pledged" to the notion of barring slavery in U.S. territories.

After denying Douglas's previous charges, Lincoln sprung an attack of his own, assailing Douglas's record with pointed questions such as: Did Douglas intend to support the admission of Kansas into the Union before it had enough citizens to qualify for statehood? Was it legal for "the people of a United States Territory, in any lawful way, . . . [to] exclude slavery from its limits prior to the formation of a State Constitution?"

Lincoln's debate strategy hinged on Douglas's answer to the second question. He thought he knew how Douglas would answer, and as it turned out, he guessed right. Slavery, Douglas declared, "cannot exist a day or an hour anywhere, unless it is supported by local police regulations." From there, Douglas expanded on his point: "Mr. Lincoln has heard me answer a hundred times from every stump in Illinois," Douglas said, that "the people of a Territory can, by lawful means, exclude slavery from their limits prior to the formation of a State Constitution."

Over the course of this campaign Douglas's reply came to be known as the Freeport doctrine. Lincoln felt it imperative to get Douglas to commit verbally to such a statement during one of the debates; otherwise it was likely to be "hard work to get him directly to the point." He intended to forcefully drive a wedge between Douglas and his followers in the Democratic Party, and President Buchanan and his Southern allies.

In order to get the controversial Kansas-Nebraska Act passed four years previously (1854), Douglas had pointed out over and over again that popular sovereignty, or leaving the decision about allowing slavery up to the inhabitants of a new state, would ensure that most of the United States' territory remained free. Since Buchanan and his cohorts believed that *Scott* v. *Sanford* (1857) had put an end to the idea of popular sovereignty, going on record as being in favor of it wouldn't have won Douglas any popularity contests among the Democratic leadership.

After Douglas responded to each of Lincoln's previous questions, Lincoln stopped throwing jabs and launched a haymaker right at Douglas's head, accusing Douglas of using documents in the first debate that the "slightest investigation" proved to be "wholly false."

Douglas did not falter for long in his response, coming back with an attack on the "spot resolutions" Lincoln offered while he was a congressman during the Mexican War. Douglas claimed this showed Lincoln's lack of patriotism. But Lincoln, who had started so poorly, was the consensus winner at Freeport. By the time the debates ended, Douglas seemed exhausted and had completely lost that booming, stentorian voice, which was his trademark throughout his career as a politician and orator. By contrast, Lincoln seemed positively energized by the nine debates, finishing up more strongly than he had begun.

In the end, Illinois remained a Democratic state, with a solid base of Democrats not up for election, already seated in the state senate. Although the Republicans made solid gains during the election of 1858, the Democrats held on to their majority in the Illinois State Legislature, and Douglas defeated Lincoln, re-elected with 54 percent of the vote.

How did Lincoln lose the U.S. Senate race of 1858?

American historians have long speculated about how a candidate could do so well in the debates preceding an election and still lose the way Abraham Lincoln did in 1858. The short answer is that Lincoln's opponent, Stephen A. Douglas, was a powerful incumbent who, for all of his waning power nationally (because of his final break with Southern Democrats over the question of slavery) was still a major political force with which to be reckoned. That only tells part of the story, though.

In truth, Lincoln knew the odds were against him from the outset. Not only was Douglas the incumbent, but the Democrats controlled the Illinois State Legislature, and state legislatures elected U.S. senators until the law governing those elections were changed in 1913, when senators began to be elected directly by the voting public. What's more, even though the Republicans made huge inroads in the Illinois State House (where representatives served two-year terms) during the general election, only one-third of Illinois state senators were up for re-election. Among the two-thirds who remained, the Democrats enjoyed a solid majority.

Such numbers were too much for anyone to expect to overcome realistically, and Douglas was re-elected with 54 percent of the legislative votes, versus 46 percent for Lincoln. Lincoln did his best to hide his disappointment at losing national office yet again. He also did his best to shore up his supporters in the fledging Republican coalition, which really had yet to gel into a genuine political party. "I am glad I made the late race," he wrote to one of them. "It gave me a hearing on the great and durable question of the age which I could have had in no other way; and though I now sink out of view, and shall be forgotten, I believe I have made some marks which will tell for the cause of civil liberty long after I am gone." Lincoln further demonstrated how much his attitudes regarding slavery had changed over the years since he re-emerged in the political arena in 1854. "The cause of civil liberty must not be surrendered at the end of *one*, or even, one *hundred* defeats," he wrote to another supporter.

64 Did Lincoln have his eye on the presidency when he ran for the Senate?

Much has been made of the fact that Abraham Lincoln went from being a little-known (if successful) frontier lawyer to sitting in the Oval Office in just two short years. When Lincoln challenged Democratic Party stalwart Stephen A. Douglas for Douglas's Senate seat, it seemed he was embarking on a fool's errand. Douglas was a senior senator from a state that enjoyed solid Democratic majorities among its registered voters.

The so-called conventional wisdom among many who have studied Lincoln's career has been that Lincoln had his eye on the presidency even as he was running for the Senate in 1858. At the time, some political commentators remarked on the possibility that Lincoln might be destined for high elective office. One such prognosticator wrote in a Massachusetts paper, the *Lowell Journal and Courier*, that Lincoln's words during his debates with Douglas had so captured the nation's imagination that many were "now calculating his fitness and chances for a more elevated position."

During his debates with Douglas, Lincoln commented candidly about his political prospects to reporter Henry Villard. Interestingly, Lincoln told Villard that while he wasn't certain how effective he might be as a senator, his wife (much to Lincoln's amusement) was convinced that he was destined for the presidency. Villard later recorded how Lincoln laughed uproariously at the thought. "Just think," he said, "of such a sucker as me as President."

During the 1859 campaign season Lincoln appeared throughout the Midwest, trying to keep Douglas from forming a coalition of centrist Democrats and conservative former Whigs in order to steal the national elections of 1860. Wherever Lincoln went, fanfare followed him. Papers such as the *Illinois Gazette*, the *Olney Times* (Illinois), the *Rockford Republican* (Illinois), the *New York Herald*, and the *Reading Journal* (Pennsylvania) all began calling at one time or another for Lincoln's presidential candidacy soon after he lost the 1858 election to Douglas. The *Olney Times* even made the call for Lincoln as president a permanent addition to the newspaper's masthead!

When the editor of the *Rock Island Register* (Illinois) added his voice to those calling for Lincoln to be elected president, Lincoln wrote him frankly, saying, "I must, in candor, say I do not think myself fit for the Presidency."

It is pretty clear that Lincoln ran for the Senate in 1858 without necessarily having an eye for the presidency. In 1859, he admitted in writing that he did not think himself capable of doing the chief executive's job. What happened between 1859 and 1860 to change Abraham Lincoln's mind on that point is another story.

65 — "Stealing" the Republican nomination for the presidency

Did Lincoln somehow steal the nomination for presidency at the 1860 Republican National Convention in Chicago? The short answer here is no, he didn't. Nevertheless, many people seem to think Lincoln was a so-called dark-horse candidate. There is an old story running through historical circles that claims Abraham Lincoln had his campaign representatives make backroom deals with the other Republican presidential candidates, playing men like William H. Seward and Salmon P. Chase against each other to secure the nomination for himself.

The truth is somewhat more complicated. In the first place, Lincoln's participation in the debates of the 1858 senatorial campaign had given him name recognition nationally. What's more, newspapers across the nation carried the Lincoln-Douglas debates and Lincoln's Cooper Union address of the previous year (given on Seward's home turf in New York City). Not to mention that the 1860 Republican National Convention took place at Chicago, in Lincoln's home state of Illinois. These factors made Lincoln something more than a dark-horse candidate.

With regard to backroom deals, Lincoln's correspondence, along with that of his lieutenants in Chicago, sheds some light on this question. (Lincoln himself stayed away from the convention in order to avoid the appearance of impropriety.) Lincoln's unofficial campaign manager was David Davis, whom Lincoln had worked with on the Illinois Circuit Court routes. (Lincoln appointed him to the United States Supreme Court in 1862.) At one point, Davis wrote: "Mr.

Lincoln is committed to no one on earth in relation to office—He promised nothing to gain his nomination, and has promised nothing." Lincoln himself said: "The responsible position assigned me, comes without conditions, save only such honorable ones as are fairly implied."

Lincoln did, however, offer spots in his cabinet to William H. Seward and Seward's great lifelong rival, Salmon P. Chase (close behind Seward as the prohibitive favorite going into the convention), as well as to Simon Cameron, because he understood his position as the first Republican chief executive was a tenuous one, requiring the support of the new regional organizations that were backing the still-forming Republican Party. Thus it was important for Lincoln to have Seward (New York), Chase (Ohio), and Cameron (Pennsylvania) in his cabinet as much for the regions they represented (and their relative leadership positions in said regions) as for who they were. In Cameron's case, Lincoln came to regret his decision. But more on that later.

66 The election of 1860

During the election of 1860 the last national institution in America cracked and splintered under increasing sectional pressure over the twin questions of states' rights and slavery. The institution in question was the Democratic Party, and the immediate beneficiary of its demise was Abraham Lincoln of Illinois.

Lincoln spent most of the campaign season sitting at home. He had made his positions on any number of election issues so well known over the previous several years that campaign advisors such as David Davis insisted it was best for Lincoln to keep his mouth shut, and not risk alienating any voters who had yet to make up their minds.

Stephen A. Douglas had spent so much of the late 1850s distancing himself from extreme members of the Democratic Party's Southern wing that he faced open rebellion at the party's convention (where he expected to be nominated for the presidency). Douglas had hoped to preserve his support in the North by doing this, but his attempt to be all things to all people finally failed. In 1860 the Democratic Party split into two wings: The Northern Democrats nominated Douglas as expected; the Southern Democrats nominated Senator John Breckinridge of Kentucky; and another splinter group, the Constitutional Union Party, nominated John Bell.

This scenario played out predictably in the general election. Lincoln won both the popular and electoral votes, beating Douglas in the popular vote by a telling margin: 1,866,452 votes to Douglas's 1,376,957. Had Douglas been able to count on either Breckinridge's 849,781 votes or on Bell's 588,879 votes, he would have easily won the popular vote. He might have also erased his dismal showing in the electoral balloting, where he came in fourth, with twelve (the only state Douglas won outright was Missouri). Lincoln won with 180 electoral votes, carrying every one of the free states save New Jersey, which he split with Douglas.

Breckinridge and Bell took all of the slave state votes, with Bell winning most of the Upper South and Breckinridge garnering the Deep South. Not only did Lincoln fail to win a single slave state, he failed to get a single vote. Is it any surprise that civil war followed such an obvious sectional split?

This reality was not lost on Lincoln, even before the election. As he came to recognize it was increasingly likely that he would win the general election, and the enormity of the task before him began to weigh on him, Lincoln told an acquaintance: "I declare to you this morning, General, that for personal considerations I would rather have a full term in the Senate—a place in which I would feel more consciously able to make a reputation, and less danger of losing it—than four years of the presidency."

67 — Why did Lincoln grow his beard?

Many people have heard the story about the young girl who told Abraham Lincoln why he ought to grow his trademark beard. Not everyone knows the particulars of the story, or that it is, in fact, true.

An eleven-year-old girl named Grace Bedell from Westfield, New York, wrote Lincoln shortly after his nomination for president in 1860, and told him he would look more distinguished and might be more easily elected if he grew a beard. He wrote her a lighthearted and friendly letter back, saying he might try it, but made no promises.

On his way to Washington, D.C., to be sworn in as president, his train stopped in Westfield, and he met Grace for the first time. Here is a newspaper account of that meeting from the *New York World* of February 19, 1861:

> *At Westfield an interesting incident occurred. Shortly after his nomination Mr. Lincoln had received from that place a letter from a little girl, who urged him, as a means of improving his personal appearance, to wear whiskers. Mr. Lincoln at the time replied, stating that although he was obliged by the suggestion, he feared his habits of life were too fixed to admit of even so slight a change as that which letting his beard grow involved. To-day, on reaching the place, he related the incident, and said that if that young lady was in the crowd he should be glad to see her. There was a momentary commotion, in the midst of which an old man, struggling through the crowd, approached, leading his daughter, a girl of apparently twelve or thirteen years of age, whom he introduced to Mr. Lincoln as his Westfield correspondent.*

Mr. Lincoln stooped down and kissed the child, and talked with her for some minutes. Her advice had not been thrown away upon the rugged chieftain. A beard of several months' growth covers (perhaps adorns) the lower part of his face. The young girl's peachy cheek must have been tickled with a stiff whisker, for the growth of which she was herself responsible.

68 Lincoln's remarks regarding secession and abolition while president-elect

Once Lincoln had won the presidency, he had to wait until March of the following year to take office. During that time he got ready for the move from his home in Springfield to the White House. He also conferred with his army of advisors (few of whom were truly intimates of his) over such questions as to who would get which post in his cabinet and how plum political postings would be distributed among the Republican Party's faithful.

As things began to unravel in the South and the sitting president (Buchanan) deplored the secession of states such as South Carolina and Georgia while claiming that he was powerless to stop them from leaving the Union, Lincoln attempted to hold his tongue on slavery and secession. Initially, he hoped that by keeping his own counsel on abolitionism and the secession crisis he might give cooler heads a chance to prevail. So when visitors came to his law offices in Springfield, he spent most of his time with them telling funny story after funny story.

But too many months intervened between Lincoln's election victory and his inauguration in 1861. He couldn't remain silent indefinitely, and so he asked Illinois senator Lyman Trumbull to include a few lines in a speech Trumbull was giving to show that Lincoln thought secessionists were few in number and the majority of the Southern people did not truly support them. Of those Southerners who did favor secession, Lincoln mistakenly wrote that they were "now in hot haste to get out of the Union, precisely because they perceive they can not, much longer, maintain apprehension among the Southern people that their homes, and firesides, and lives, are to be endangered by the action of the Federal Government." From there Lincoln went on to make the following astonishing statement: "I am rather glad of this military preparation in the South. It will enable the people the more easily to suppress any uprisings there, which their misrepresentation of purposes may have encouraged." Trumbull decided against including these lines, and history has shown it was a good thing that he did.

Initially, Lincoln completely misjudged the intent of those leading the secession movement in the South and the level of support they enjoyed in their respective states. To Lincoln, the threat of secession, followed by the actuality of it, was merely the latest in a series of bluffs perpetrated by Southern politicians that dated all the way back to the Revolution. To his thinking, Southern leaders weren't really aiming to leave the country, they were putting leverage on him to change his government, and on that point Lincoln adamantly refused to budge.

When Missouri senator John J. Crittenden proposed a new compromise that would extend the Missouri Compromise line out to the California state border and call for strenuous enforcement of the Fugitive Slave Law, Lincoln did not give it a warm reception. "I will suffer death," he said with uncharacteristic bluntness, "before I will consent or will advise my friend to consent to any concession or compromise which looks like buying the privilege to take possession of this government to which we have a constitutional right."

On balance, Lincoln did also make clear that he intended to do nothing to curb slavery where it already legally existed. However, his assurances fell on deaf ears. Southerners believed that Lincoln intended to foist upon them a political and social system that effectively ended their own cherished one. They acted accordingly, and the bloody result was the American Civil War.

69 Goats in the White House?

Not only did Lincoln keep goats at the White House, his son Willie had a pony there, which he rode daily. Lincoln was one of the youngest presidents up to that point, and he had started a family late in life, so his young children were a novelty in the White House.

As a result, both Willie and Tad were inundated with presents. Not least of these were a pony for Willie, a turkey named Jack (more on him later), and two goats named Nanny and Nanko for Tad. Both boys (but Tad especially) liked to hitch one or the other of these goats up to a makeshift cart contrived of a kitchen chair and harness. Then the boys would have the goat in question pull them up and down the halls of the executive mansion.

On one memorable occasion, Tad rode one of these goat carts right through a formal reception in one of the large meeting rooms, whooping and hollering as several of the ladies in attendance pulled up their hoop skirts to make way for him. Obviously the Lincoln family took parenting no more seriously in Washington, D.C., than they had back in Springfield, because the boys frequently ran amok like this. What's more, on those odd occasions when Lincoln could join them, he would do so. Lincoln loved roughhousing with his boys and could even be found playing with them out on the White House lawn.

As for Jack, the turkey, he had been a gift to the Lincolns intended for their Thanksgiving dinner. Tad taught the turkey to follow him around and grew attached to the bird, so much so that when the time came for the bird to be killed, Tad interrupted one of Lincoln's cabinet meetings and cried and pleaded so relentlessly that Lincoln at length signed a "stay of execution" for the poor bird.

Later on, during one of the elections where the White House doubled as a polling place for the Pennsylvania regiment posted on the executive mansion's south lawn, Jack made his way into the line of soldiers waiting for their time in the polls. Lincoln saw this and asked his son whether Jack planned to vote. "He is under age," Tad replied.

Part 4

Lincoln and the Civil War

Many historians have categorized Abraham Lincoln as the Union's greatest single asset in the War Between the States. Did you know Lincoln ignored the civil rights of some citizens during the war? In this section, you'll pick up some diverse details, including what Lincoln meant when he said he had "a pumpkin in each bag," and how many generals Lincoln had to go through before he found one who was a match for Robert E. Lee on the battlefield. Just what type of wartime chief executive was Lincoln? Here, you'll find out.

December 1860:
The South Carolinian secession crisis

70

Less than a week after Abraham Lincoln won the presidential election of 1860, the South Carolina legislature called for a convention to discuss secession. Like many other politicians, Lincoln thought this move was a bluff. After all, Southerners had been threatening to secede from the Union for decades, wresting concession after concession from Northerners over the institution of slavery. On December 20, the convention proved Lincoln and so many others wrong, voting overwhelmingly for secession.

Even after South Carolina voted to secede, Lincoln refused to believe that Southerners were serious about dissolving the Union. He privately expressed the sentiment that it might be good finally to get the question of slavery out of the way. Realistically, there was precious little Lincoln could do about it until his inauguration during the first week of March in 1861. That task fell to outgoing president James Buchanan, a Northerner with Southern sympathies.

Buchanan took an odd position. He believed that although no state had the right to dissolve its ties to the Union without the consent of the federal government, the federal government had no power to stop any state that took this drastic step. Andrew Jackson, a Southern Democrat and slaveholder himself, had stemmed the tide of South Carolinian secession talk in 1832 by sending in federal troops to occupy the South Carolina State Militia's armories. He also twisted the arms of their congressional delegation until they went back to negotiating a compromise over the tariff they had so bitterly protested.

On his end, Lincoln hoped that by keeping his mouth shut (for the most part), he could allow Southern secession talk to die of its own accord, doing nothing to fan the flames of disunion in other Southern states. New York senator William H. Seward (already tabbed as Lincoln's presumptive secretary of state) agreed with this strategy. Seward believed that the key to dealing with this crisis was to do nothing to provoke secessionist movements in the Upper South states such as Virginia and Maryland, where Unionists still controlled the state legislatures.

Lincoln subscribed to that position, especially since Buchanan had stood by idly while Southern forces had seized Union fort after Union fort and Federal armory after Federal armory in their own territory. Assuming that he would have a real shooting war on his hands once he took office, Lincoln would be starting nearly from scratch in his quest to preserve the Union and pacify those parts of the country then in rebellion—if he could even hold on to the states of the Upper South.

71 Was there a plot to kill Lincoln before he took office in 1861?

As Lincoln made his way to Washington for his March 1861 inauguration, he received word that Southern sympathizers were planning his murder during a train change in Baltimore, Maryland. Allan Pinkerton (who later became coordinator of Lincoln's intelligence-gathering services during the war) warned that a barber named Cypriano Ferrandini and several compatriots intended to kill Lincoln as he came through a particularly narrow portion of the Calvert Street Station. Pinkerton was head of his own detective agency, hired by the president of the Philadelphia, Wilmington & Baltimore Railroad. The president of the railroad was worried that in the course of trying to kill Lincoln, Southern agents might damage railroad property (by blowing up a bridge, for example).

After a hasty council of war (with Lincoln initially balking at changing his schedule as a concession to concerns over his safety), Lincoln's handlers decided that he must pass through Baltimore at night, in disguise. He would travel with only his trusted friend (and budding bodyguard), big, brawling Illinois lawyer Ward Hill Lamon and Pinkerton himself as his companions. And so it went. Lincoln changed trains in Baltimore in the middle of the night without incident.

This is not to say that Lincoln did not pay a price for taking the precaution of changing his schedule. Lincoln had doffed his trademark stovepipe hat in favor of a soft cloth cap, but somehow, the newspapers wrote that Lincoln opted for a Scottish plaid cap and military coat. As such, Lincoln was the butt of much ridicule, and his courage was called into question any number of times. It was not an experience he cared to repeat. There were several other attempts on Lincoln's life over the course of his presidency. Never again did he take extraordinary precautions in order to guard against them. In the end, he paid the ultimate price for his physical courage.

 ## 72 March 1861: Lincoln takes office

When a new chief executive takes office today, he has a transition support staff numbering in the hundreds. Abraham Lincoln went to work in March of 1861 with two personal secretaries and no official cabinet members. In fact, Lincoln tried to do nearly everything himself from the moment he took office onward.

One of the hardest-working U.S. presidents, Lincoln rose early, and after a meager breakfast, he headed right to his office. Writing out correspondence, answering letters, meeting with office-seekers, trying to come to grips with secession problems in the Deep South, and figuring out what to do about South Carolina's blockade of Fort Sumter in Charleston Harbor . . . it was all in a day's work.

But it was simply too much for one man to do, even with the help of his two secretaries, John Nicolay and John Hay, and eventually he borrowed the services of a clerk who was ostensibly assigned to the War Department, using him liberally to take dictation, respond to correspondence, and so forth.

If, as he later remarked, Lincoln "was entirely ignorant not only of the duties, but of the manner of doing the business" required of a sitting president when he came to office in March of 1861, Lincoln was partly saved by his experience with the business of government (albeit mostly at the state legislative level). He adapted quickly, and by sheer necessity began to work more efficiently on the daily work associated with being president. It was a good thing he did. Fort Sumter needed to be either resupplied or evacuated, and that thorny first military problem of the coming secession war would require vast amounts of Lincoln's attention.

Fort Sumter

Abraham Lincoln's response to the initial crisis of his presidency was disorganized, inconsistent, and inadequate. The question that plagued him was whether and how to resupply or reinforce Fort Sumter, a U.S. Army base protecting the harbor entrance in Charleston, South Carolina. This problem haunted Lincoln from the day he was inaugurated until the day South Carolina artillery shelling forced Major Robert Anderson, Sumter's commander, to surrender along with his entire command.

At least in part, Lincoln dithered and vacillated over what to do about Fort Sumter. But that's because he wanted to establish a credible historical record of not antagonizing Southern secessionists without also backing down from his inauguration pledge that he would defend and hold Union military facilities where they already existed. In other words, Lincoln was playing a dangerous game.

Also, Lincoln's cabinet was bitterly divided on the question of what to do about Sumter. Secretary of State William Seward had made a foolish move by independently (and without presidential approval) promising several Confederate officials that there would be no attempt to reinforce Fort Sumter. He strongly recommended that Fort Sumter simply be abandoned to the Confederate forces then surrounding it. He further insisted that if there was so much as an attempt to resupply the beleaguered fort, then Lincoln's administration must first notify South Carolina's government that a fleet was underway to resupply the fort, and only that fort, in their harbor. Because he was building a case for his administration's careful attempts at securing a peaceful resolution to the secession crisis, Lincoln agreed to this approach, sealing Sumter's fate by forfeiting the element of surprise.

Lincoln was also treading carefully on the Fort Sumter issue because several states in the Upper South (namely Virginia, North Carolina, Arkansas, and Tennessee) were watching how he handled the situation. These states had Unionist majorities in the state conventions they had called to respond to the secession crisis. But it was well known that if the federal government attempted to use force to coerce the states of the Deep South back into the Union, it would not play well in the states of the Upper South.

Once the fleet sent to resupply Fort Sumter was spotted off the South Carolina coast, South Carolina militia units on the Charleston shore opened fire on Anderson's command. After a thirty-three-hour bombardment, Anderson was no longer able to resist. He surrendered the fort to South Carolina's militia on April 14, 1861. After Anderson did so, Lincoln remarked that Sumter had served its purpose: A civil war had begun in earnest, and shots had been fired, but Lincoln had not ordered the first shots.

Lincoln's (and Seward's) hope, that steering a conciliatory course would keep the states of the Upper South in the Union, was dashed by the secession of Virginia, Tennessee, North Carolina, and Arkansas, following Lincoln's call for troops from each state's militia levees to help pacify the Southern states then in rebellion. The Civil War had begun.

 ## 74 "Keep your friends close, but your enemies closer"

Because the Republican Party in 1860 was really a political party in name only, Abraham Lincoln's position as head of that party was pretty uncertain. The Republican Party was a still-forming coalition of a variety of regional interests. Lincoln needed men who commanded the collective loyalty of these disparate groups to bind the party more closely together. This became especially important after most of the Southern states seceded and hostilities broke out between the North and the South.

Seen in this light, the list of cabinet members Lincoln eventually came up with is unsurprising. William H. Seward (New York) was named secretary of state; Salmon P. Chase (Ohio) became secretary of the treasury; Simon Cameron (Pennsylvania) assumed the position of secretary of war; and Edward

Bates (a former Whig from the border state of Missouri) became attorney general. All four of these men had been Lincoln's rivals for the Republican presidential nomination, and their support was crucial to Lincoln during his first few months in office. With sectional concerns still in mind, Lincoln set about rounding out his cabinet by appointing Caleb B. Smith (Indiana) as secretary of the interior, Gideon V. Welles (Connecticut) as secretary of the navy, and Montgomery Blair (District of Columbia) as postmaster general.

Because he was using his cabinet as a compromise model in hopes of binding both his political party and his nation more closely together, Lincoln was willing to sacrifice harmony within his cabinet in favor of having men who could sell his programs to their constituents. It was a choice he would come to regret. Seward and Chase, rivals within the party, despised each other. Seward also believed (at least initially) that Lincoln was a simple backwoods lawyer. And so Seward thought it would be no problem for him to act as a sort of premier, ruling through a compliant Lincoln, who would gratefully sign off on Seward's policies. With that in mind, Seward proved highly meddlesome, butting into the workings of other executive-branch departments without invitation.

For his part, Chase did everything he could to sabotage Seward. This included leaking the particulars of supposedly private conversations held during cabinet meetings to members of the radical wing of the Republican delegation to Congress. These worthies, sufficiently incensed by the "facts" that Chase saw fit to feed them, began to clamor for Seward's resignation as secretary of state.

At one point, they succeeded. But Lincoln refused to accept that resignation and invited the loudest members of the congressional Radical Republicans to a meeting at the executive mansion late one night in December 1862. Imagine their surprise when they learned that Lincoln had called his entire cabinet (with the exception of Seward) to the same meeting! Once all were present, Lincoln informed the congressional delegation that far from being at each others' throats, his cabinet members got along very well. He then had each member of the cabinet stand and corroborate his statement.

This left Chase in a real bind. Either he could stand and say that he agreed with the president and make himself look like a liar to his allies among the radicals, or he could disagree publicly with the president and in all likelihood be dismissed from his post. After some waffling, Chase reluctantly agreed with Lincoln, thereby damaging his own credibility with the radicals.

The next day Chase tendered his own resignation to Lincoln, who exhibited great delight in having it, then quickly dismissed Chase from his presence, but not from his post. Lincoln remarked upon receiving Chase's letter of resignation that he had "a pumpkin in each bag," meaning he was balanced out. If the Radical Republicans wanted Seward gone, there was nothing to stop Lincoln from publicly accepting Chase's written resignation and booting him from the cabinet as well, something the radicals were ill-prepared to accept, regardless of Chase's recent loss of face with them.

From this point onward, Chase's days as treasury secretary were numbered. Also, after this episode it was clear to Seward that he owed his continued tenure as secretary of state to Lincoln and Lincoln alone. Understanding this, Seward fell into line, becoming one of Lincoln's more trusted cabinet members.

Later in Lincoln's first term, Supreme Court Chief Justice Roger B. Taney died, which left a post open. Lincoln knew that for all of his vanity, egotism, and scheming, Salmon P. Chase revered the Constitution and the institution of the Supreme Court. By appointing Chase as chief justice, Lincoln rid himself of a problematic appointment while at the same time securing an able (and abolitionist) chief justice who would make sure that no challenge arose to the legality of the Thirteenth, Fourteenth, and Fifteenth amendments to the Constitution.

Where Seward and Chase feuded incessantly, Simon Cameron presented a completely different problem as secretary of war. When Lincoln initially considered appointing Cameron to his cabinet, members of the Republican Party in Cameron's home state of Pennsylvania had warned Lincoln repeatedly about Cameron's corruption. Lincoln vacillated over the question of whether to include Cameron in his cabinet, eventually deciding that Cameron was too valuable to him in Pennsylvania to be left out.

While Cameron himself turned out to be personally honest, he was a dreadful administrator. Like Warren G. Harding a generation later, he had trouble keeping his own friends from dipping their snouts in the public trough. He awarded military supply contracts without taking bids. Goods were ordered and paid for, but never delivered, with contractors pocketing the payments. Eventually things got so bad that Lincoln informed Cameron that he would like to grant Cameron's wish of becoming ambassador to Russia—all Cameron had to do was resign as war secretary.

The problem was, Cameron had no desire to go to Russia and became downright tearful at the thought of losing his cabinet-level post. But with the war going badly, Lincoln continued to jockey with Cameron, and by January of 1862, he got Cameron's resignation.

The man who replaced Cameron was a star trial lawyer from Pittsburgh. Edwin McMasters Stanton had been attorney general under the previous administration and knew Lincoln slightly from an aborted attempt to work on a case together back in the mid-1850s (the arrogant little Stanton repeatedly referred to Lincoln as a monkey). Lincoln had been so impressed with Stanton's work transitioning the office of attorney general over from the Buchanan administration that he now offered Stanton the post of secretary of war. It was a bold move, which paid off in spades. Stanton became Lincoln's only true intimate in his contentious cabinet!

75 Illegally jailing political dissenters?

Did Lincoln really do that? Washington, D.C., sits between Virginia (a state that seceded from the Union in April 1861) and Maryland (a slave state and a so-called border state between the North and the South). Lincoln simply could not afford to have Maryland decamp from the Union along with the states of the Upper South, which left in the second wave of secession after the fall of Fort Sumter in mid-April 1861. If that happened, then the national capital would be a Federal island in a Confederate sea.

With this idea in mind, Lincoln authorized the suspension of the writ of habeas corpus (the right to a speedy trial) in the state of Maryland. Empowered by this action, Union military officials could jail anyone they considered to be aiding or abetting the Confederate cause, and they could do so for an indefinite period of time, without either charging the person in question with a crime or bringing him to trial.

Lincoln did not take this action lightly. He did, however, realize that Baltimore (and by association, the entire eastern portion of the state) was home to an overwhelmingly pro-Southern population. After all, a plot had been hatched in Baltimore to assassinate Lincoln on his way to his inauguration. What's more, once hostilities had broken out, civic leaders in Baltimore (through their governor, Thomas Hicks, and Baltimore mayor George W. Brown) had first petitioned the president on April 18, 1861, asking him to march any reinforcements of Federal troops garrisoning in Washington, D.C., around (rather than through) the city of Baltimore. Lincoln had agreed, albeit hesitantly, saying in what must have seemed a joking manner: "If I grant you this concession, that no troops shall pass through the city, you will be back here to-morrow demanding that none shall be marched around it."

Emboldened by Lincoln's initial acquiescence on this point, four days later these same civic leaders came to Lincoln and insisted that he bypass Maryland altogether, that he make peace with the Confederacy at any cost, and that he appoint the British ambassador to the United States to negotiate a cease-fire. By this point, Lincoln had had quite enough of being accommodating. "You would have me break my oath and surrender the government without a blow," he exclaimed. "There is no Washington in that—no Jackson in that—no manhood nor honor in that." When Lincoln suspended the writ of habeas corpus in Maryland, he knew precisely what he was doing and could justify its necessity, at least in his own mind.

When Congress reconvened in the summer of 1861, the only one of Lincoln's extraconstitutional actions that even raised a congressional eyebrow was his suspension of the writ in Maryland. However, most who spoke out on either side of this troubling issue referred to it as did Senator John Sherman of Ohio: "I approve the action of the President. . . . He did precisely what I would have done if I had been in his place—no more, no less; but I cannot here, in my place, as a Senator, under oath, declare that what he did do was . . . strictly legal, and in consonance with the provisions of the Constitution."

Lincoln could not, however, escape the court system on this point. Supreme Court Chief Justice Roger B. Taney (a Maryland man, and the author of the hated Dred Scott decision) issued a writ of habeas corpus in the case of John Merryman, a company-grade officer in a Southern-leaning drill company. In a ruling known as *Ex Parte Merryman*, Taney insisted that Lincoln must either charge and try this young man or release him. Lincoln had previously demonstrated his disregard for Taney's rulings when he simply ignored the Dred Scott decision, but this time Lincoln was on thin ice constitutionally, and he knew it. But Taney had no power to execute his ruling. What's more, Maryland simply had to be kept in the Union in order to keep Washington, D.C., from falling into Southern hands.

And that is why our greatest president denied a select group of Southern-sympathizing Maryland agitators their civil rights. Should he have done it? Who can say? The fact that he did speaks volumes about how seriously Lincoln, ever the champion of the common man in the face of tyranny, took the threat of losing Maryland, and by extension the national capital, to the South.

76 Lincoln and his generals: Scott

Abraham Lincoln was three years old when Winfield Scott received his commission as a general (of volunteers) in the United States Army. Scott spent the next forty-nine years commanding troops on the battlefield in two major wars, the War of 1812 and the Mexican War, to say nothing of his involvement in countless Indian wars. In 1852 Scott hoped to follow in the footsteps of his Mexican War colleague (and rival) Zachary Taylor by winning election as a Whig to the presidency. As it turned out, Scott was the last Whig Party candidate for president, and, like the party that was dying even as it nominated him, Scott ran a lackluster campaign. He was trounced at the polls, losing in a landslide to Democrat Franklin Pierce.

By the outbreak of the American Civil War, Scott was in his midseventies and weighed over 300 pounds. Hobbled by gout, Scott could no longer mount a horse and was obviously incapable of leading troops in the field. He had lost none of his highly touted capacity for concocting sound military strategy, though. Scott was the father of the so-called Anaconda Plan, which called for a Union blockade of the Confederacy by seizing control of the Mississippi River and using several large Union armies to squeeze the South into submission.

Lincoln employed this plan to defeat the Confederacy once it became clear that the war would last far longer than most people on both sides of the conflict (Lincoln and Scott excepted) believed it would. Thus, Scott had an impact on

Union war policy long after he resigned and went into retirement. For Lincoln, it was all a question of finding men capable of executing Scott's grand strategy.

Knowing that he was long past his prime as a battlefield commander, Scott recommended that his former chief of staff (and fellow Virginian) Robert E. Lee be offered the overall command of the Union army. Scott was understandably disappointed when Lee refused the offer, resigned his commission, and joined the still-forming Confederate army.

Scott was convinced that the conquest of the South would take years and cost thousands of lives. Thus, he was so unconcerned with the outcome of Bull Run, the war's first large-scale battle, that when Lincoln himself called on Scott for an update on the battle's progress, Scott was taking his customary afternoon nap.

By November of 1861, Lincoln had realized it was time for a more hands-on commander. He accepted the offer of resignation that Scott had tendered and left standing earlier that same year.

Within twenty-four hours, George B. McClellan had been recalled from West Virginia in order to succeed Scott. McClellan brought a whole slew of headaches for his commander-in-chief.

77 Bull Run: Make way for a new commander

Bull Run, or Manassas, as it was also called, was the first major engagement of the American Civil War. It was both an unqualified logistical nightmare and a full-blown military disaster for the North. Although the contest could have gone either way, the South won because of reinforcements arriving literally at the last minute. This contributed to the ongoing myth of Southern military superiority on the battlefield, something that haunted many a soldier in the Army of the Potomac until Ulysses S. Grant arrived on the scene two years later.

Mostly, Bull Run can be chalked up as a rookie mistake on the Northern side of the tally sheet, and as rookie luck on the Southern side. Both sides suffered the problems inexperienced combat groups suffer. They lacked strong leadership at the company level; each side had logistical problems due to lack of clear-cut supply lines. Plus, countless green troops faltered under withering enemy fire, trying to follow the orders of equally green commanders.

Lincoln was not immune from rookie mistakes either, having allowed pressure from Congress and the Northern media to sway him into insisting on a military confrontation as an answer to a political problem. But Lincoln learned his lesson at Bull Run, and never again insisted baldly that troops move in response to editorials in the *New York Tribune*. He also realized he had raw recruits who could barely march, where he needed a professional army. To accomplish this, Lincoln demoted McDowell and ushered Army General Winfield Scott into long overdue retirement, making way for a new commander who could build an army that would defeat the South and give Lincoln a political solution on the battlefield.

 78 Lincoln and his generals: McClellan

On the same day Union troops were routed at Bull Run, Abraham Lincoln called upon a young general who was having success against the Confederates in a series of small engagements in what is now West Virginia. George Brinton McClellan was an Ohio native in his mid-thirties, a West Point graduate (near the top of his class), and by all accounts a good engineer. He had been sent to Russia to act as an observer during the Crimean War in the late 1850s, then had resigned his commission to take a job running the Illinois Central Railroad (a client of Lincoln's during the same period).

Lincoln met with McClellan, and within days had made him overall commander of the Union forces in the east. (McClellan would not take command of all Union armies until November of 1861, upon General Scott's retirement.)

McClellan went to work building the mass of state militia levees into a proper army. He turned out to be more than adequate for the task. A superb organizer and relentlessly consistent drill master, he knew exactly what needed to be done to create what eventually became his most lasting legacy: the Army of the Potomac. The problem with McClellan wasn't that he couldn't organize and train an army. The problem was his refusal to do anything with said army once he had built it.

McClellan failed the good soldier/good general test: To be a good soldier, you must love the army. McClellan clearly did that, and his army clearly loved him back. However, a good general must be willing to kill the thing he loves, if necessary to achieve a victory. McClellan simply could not bear to put his army into jeopardy.

To make matters worse, McClellan quickly developed a persecution complex. Add his already outsized ego to the mix (he had earned his nickname "Little Napoleon"), and it was hardly a winning combination. When senators prodded him about why he was dithering away the 1862 campaign season instead of attacking Lee's smaller Army of Northern Virginia, McClellan claimed he needed to wait until more bridges were built across the Potomac to secure his lines of retreat. Once they were finished examining McClellan, one of the examiners, Zachariah Chandler, said, "I don't know much about war, but it seems to me that this is infernal, unmitigated cowardice."

Lincoln's own relationship with McClellan started out strongly enough, but later faltered because of McClellan's outsized ego. In the spring of 1862, Lincoln relieved McClellan of his duties as overall commander of the Union armies so that McClellan could focus on using the Army of the Potomac to corner and defeat Lee and the Army of Northern Virginia. After the costly and inconclusive Peninsular campaign, Lincoln shifted the majority of McClellan's troops to General John Pope's command. But once Pope blundered badly at the second battle of Bull Run, Lincoln had little alternative other than to return McClellan to his command.

This move did nothing to impede McClellan's belief in his own infallibility. After McClellan's characteristic lack of decisiveness led him to a draw with Lee at Antietam, when he had his Southern adversary at a tactical disadvantage, Lincoln again was forced to remove McClellan from command. McClellan went home to New Jersey, sure that he would again be recalled after his latest successor (Ambrose E. Burnside) blundered (which he quickly did at Fredericksburg). But that recall never came. McClellan was finished as a battlefield commander.

 **79 Antietam**

During the summer of 1862, General Robert E. Lee launched what later became known as his "invasion of the North," in hopes of taking the war to his adversaries, as opposed to fighting a continued defensive action in his beloved Virginia. Lee further hoped to end the war quickly by encircling and cutting off Washington, D.C.

Opposing Lee was that excellent builder of armies, George Brinton McClellan. Late in the campaign season of 1862, Lee's marching orders for the Maryland campaign fell into Union hands. McClellan for once moved quickly, attacking Lee in western Maryland, blunting his advance. After forcing Lee into retreat, the Army of the Potomac advanced from the battle site at South Mountain toward a showdown at the city of Sharpsburg. Rolling into Sharpsburg on September 16, 1862, McClellan found Lee's forces drawn up on a hill on the southern side of Antietam Creek. The single bloodiest engagement of the war followed.

Once again McClellan moved slowly, unsure of whether Lee was waiting to spring a trap. Lee was badly outnumbered and had his back to the Potomac. It would take time to re-cross the river in order to slip back into Virginia. Lee was outnumbered by almost two to one; whereas McClellan held some of his troops in reserve, Lee committed all of his forces to the first day's fighting, and the Army of Northern Virginia fought the Federals to a draw. However, Lee had taken the high ground, so when the Army of the Potomac advanced across that creek on the second day of the battle, Lee's men concentrated their murderous fire on the only bridge where the Union troops could cross. Climbing over the bodies of their dead comrades, General Ambrose Burnside's men swept across a new-mown cornfield, which offered them no cover. They attacked the Confederate soldiers on the top of the hill overlooking Antietam Creek again and again, giving as good as they got, but the stubborn resistance of Lee's men forced them to withdraw. On the single bloodiest day of the Civil War (September 17, 1862), Union losses totaled 12,410, while the Confederates lost 10,700 men. This casualty rate was greater than the number of American soldiers killed in every battle in every war ever fought by Americans *combined* up to that point.

Reeling from losses he could ill afford, Lee still managed to slip across the Potomac after a third day of fighting, which was little more than a series of skirmishes with the overcautious McClellan. Rather than harry Lee during his river crossing, McClellan let him go.

The battle of Antietam, as it was known in the North (Southerners referred to it as Sharpsburg, after the village outside which it took place), had two long-term effects on both American history and on President Abraham Lincoln's career. First, it signaled the beginning of the end of Lincoln's second experiment with George B. McClellan as both his principal battlefield commander and head of the Union army. Second, although technically a draw, it was hailed in the North as a victory because Lee's army was forced to withdraw after a failed invasion of the North. Lincoln used news of this "victory" to push for, and get support for his Emancipation Proclamation of 1863.

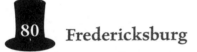

80 Fredericksburg

"I hope it is not so bad as all that."

—Abraham Lincoln, upon receiving word of the
Federal disaster at the battle of Frederickburg

It wasn't. It was worse. One out of every ten soldiers in the Army of the Potomac died at the battle of Fredericksburg (the death toll reached 12,600 for the Union, out of a force that numbered 113,000). After learning the full details of the disaster, Lincoln said, "If there is a worse place than Hell, I am in it."

In November 1862, Lincoln had fired George B. McClellan as commander of the Army of the Potomac. In December of that same year, that same army, under new commanding general Ambrose E. Burnside, attempted to cross the Rappahannock River in northern Virginia and attack Robert E. Lee's troops. The Confederates were entrenched in the heights overlooking the hamlet of Fredericksburg.

Burnside's troops encountered fierce resistance from the outset. Having taken Fredericksburg itself, Burnside sent his men scampering uphill in a two-pronged assault toward the ridge where Lee's army was dug in. The assault on the left failed utterly, although a division commanded by George G. Meade temporarily broke through the lines Confederate general Thomas J. "Stonewall" Jackson commanded. Meade received no support, though, and was quickly forced to retreat.

On the right wing, rebel troops under General James Longstreet had the approach to their position on Marye's Heights (another name for Fredericksburg) so well covered that, as one of Longstreet's officers put it, "A chicken could not live on that field when we open on it." Seven times the Union lines advanced straight into the teeth of withering fire from the Confederate positions. Of this endeavor one Union soldier said, "We might as well have tried to take Hell."

Headlines in Northern papers screamed out the news of the latest Union military catastrophe. A correspondent for *Harper's Weekly* wrote that the American people "have borne, silently and grimly, imbecility, treachery, failure, privation, loss of friends and means, almost every suffering which can afflict a brave people. But they cannot be expected to suffer that such massacres as this at Fredericksburg shall be repeated."

Lincoln had more fallout from the Fredericksburg debacle than he had bargained for. At this point, several Radical Republican senators (secretly egged on by Treasury Secretary Salmon P. Chase) called publicly for Secretary of State William H. Seward's resignation (see number 74). Lincoln weathered this storm and dealt brilliantly with both the radicals and the disloyal Chase, but not before complaining to a friend:

> *What do these men want? . . . They wish to get rid of me, and I am sometimes half disposed to gratify them. . . . Since I heard last night of the proceedings of the caucus [of senators who wished to replace Seward] I have been more distressed than by any event of my life. . . . We are now on the brink of destruction. It appears to me the Almighty is against us, and I can hardly see a ray of hope.*

81 The Emancipation Proclamation

When the rebel army was at Frederick, I determined, as soon as it should be driven out of Maryland, to issue a proclamation of emancipation, such as I thought most likely to be useful. I said nothing to anyone; but I made the promise to myself and to my Maker. The rebel army is now driven out, and I am going to fulfill that promise.

—**Abraham Lincoln in an address to his cabinet, September 22, 1862**

As you may recall from the point on Lincoln's abolitionism (see number 52), he made it clear during the election of 1860 and in the months preceding and following his inauguration, that he was intent on preserving the Union, regardless of his personal desire to end slavery.

Many historians have maintained that Lincoln's Emancipation Proclamation of 1863 freed not one slave. After all, his proclamation was mute on the question of slavery in those so-called border states, Southern states such as Maryland and Missouri, which had not seceded, but where slavery was legal. Lincoln's proclamation explicitly "freed" slaves only in those areas in rebellion against the federal government. Needless to say, slave owners and law enforcement officials in places such as Georgia and Alabama no longer recognized Lincoln's authority to make such a proclamation.

Many white laborers in the North feared that abolition of slavery would unleash a deluge of cheap black labor to compete with them for wages in

Northern cities. The predictable result was a number of race-related riots and violence in various Northern cities in 1862.

Interestingly, many Northern men gave slavery little if any thought at all when enlisting in the army. The majority cited a desire to help to preserve the Union that Southerners were attempting to sever. "I came out to fight for the restoration of the Union and to keep slavery [from] going into the territories & not to free the niggers," wrote one soldier in 1862. Balancing such attitudes were those of radicals on the other side of the question who insisted that Lincoln free all the slaves in America immediately.

Lincoln carried on his balancing act over the abolition of slavery for almost two years. But by the middle of the war, many of the Northern soldiers' more callous attitudes toward blacks had begun to change, thanks in large part to the first-time exposure so many Union soldiers had to black slaves. These people sheltered escaped Union prisoners of war, acted as guides and spies for the Northern armies, and rendered any number of other services to Federal troops during the war's early years.

Lincoln was aware of such minute shifts in the national attitude toward slavery and emancipation, and coupled with his perception of the political situation abroad, he realized he could use emancipation to block potential European intervention in the war. By the early 1860s there was much talk in Britain of recognizing the South as a separate country, intervening militarily, and offering to mediate a peace settlement.

In fact, one British cabinet-level minister had spoken out explicitly on that topic. Chancellor of the Exchequer (akin to the American secretary of the treasury) and future prime minister William Gladstone wrote on July 26, 1862, "It is indeed much to be desired that this bloody and purposeless conflict should cease." In a speech given at Newcastle not long afterward, Gladstone expanded on the above statement, saying that "Jefferson Davis and other leaders of the South have made an army; they are making, it appears, a navy; and they have made what is more than either, they have made a nation." For his part, British Prime Minister Lord Palmerston was more cautious, taking a wait-and-see position on the question of intervention.

None of this was lost on Lincoln. Kept well informed by Charles Francis Adams (son of John Quincy Adams and grandson of John Adams), his minister to Great Britain, Lincoln realized that if he could make the war about slavery rather than secession, the British government would lose all interest in intervention. On January 23, 1863, Charles Francis Adams's son and private secretary, Henry Adams, wrote in response to news of Lincoln's proclamation, "The Emancipation Proclamation has done more for us here than all our former victories and all our diplomacy. It is creating an almost convulsive reaction in our favor. . . . We are much encouraged and in high spirits. If only you at home don't have disasters, we will give such a checkmate to the foreign hopes of the rebels as they have never yet had."

Lincoln later regarded the Emancipation Proclamation as his administration's greatest accomplishment. It was a calculated political gamble, made in hopes that the resultant howls of those devastated by it would be balanced out by the cheers of those who had waited so long for it. As it turned out, he guessed right.

82 Which of Lincoln's children died in the White House?

On Thursday, February 20, 1862, Abraham Lincoln's third son, William Wallace ("Willie") Lincoln, died of what was probably typhoid fever. He died at age eleven in the bed that currently occupies the Lincoln Bedroom in the executive mansion—the room supposedly haunted by Lincoln's ghost. Lincoln's youngest son, Tad, also came down with the malady, and became very ill at the same time. Lincoln wore himself ragged staying up and tending to both sick boys. When Willie died, Lincoln looked at the dead child's face and said, "He was too good for this earth . . . but then we loved him so."

The boy had taken ill early in February, shortly before Mary Todd Lincoln threw a massive gala party to show off the newly refurbished White House. Periodically throughout the evening both parents had slipped away from the party to check on Willie. After he died, the child was embalmed in the Green Room at the White House, where his funeral was held, during one of the fiercest rainstorms in the capital's history.

His parents handled their grief very differently. Abraham's grief was a private thing: He would often closet himself in a room so that he could weep over his lost son. He took to quoting passages from Shakespeare's *Macbeth*, *King John*, and *King Lear*, which dealt with a parent's loss of a beloved child.

Mary stayed in bed for three weeks. She didn't even attend her son's funeral. When she did appear in public again, she was arrayed in black from top to toe, so covered in veils and lace that she was frequently unrecognizable. So profound was her sorrow (and so unstable her mental state) that Abraham Lincoln's usually outgoing and sociable wife forbade any social functions at the White House for almost a year after her son's death. There is little question that the loss of his son had an adverse effect on Lincoln's conduct as chief executive. He lacked energy and listlessly stumbled around the White House for weeks afterward. Whereas in his youth periods of depression had left him bedridden in much the same manner as his wife then was, Lincoln did not have the luxury of forgoing his responsibilities and retiring to his bed, so he bore his grief as well as he could, under the circumstances.

According to his wife, Lincoln turned to religion for the first time after Willie's death. This is probably not altogether true. Lincoln was a lifelong and confirmed skeptic about matters of organized religion, and he never joined a congregation. However, Lincoln did speak on a number of occasions with the minister of the Presbyterian Church in Washington, D.C., where his family regularly attended worship services. As historian David Herbert Donald writes in *Lincoln*:

> *During the weeks after Willie's death Lincoln had several long talks with the Reverend Phineas D. Gurley, pastor of the New York Avenue Presbyterian Church in Washington, where the Lincolns rented a pew. Gently the clergyman comforted him with the assurance that Willie was not dead but still lived in heaven. Lincoln may not have believed him, but he wished to believe him. He did not experience a religious conversion, though when he looked back on the events of that tragic spring, he recognized that he underwent what he called "a process of crystallization" in his religious*

beliefs. Even so, he did not become a member of any Christian denomination, nor did he abandon his fundamental fatalism.

83 Gettysburg

In May of 1863, General Robert E. Lee, facing the reality that the South would eventually lose a strictly defensive war, gambled heavily that a second invasion of the North would draw Federal armies into a final, climactic battle that would leave the Confederacy victorious on the battlefield. In support of this strategy, Lee's Army of Northern Virginia crossed the Potomac River, and moved quickly through Maryland, into south-central Pennsylvania.

Lee intended to attack Washington, D.C., from the north, forcing the Federal Army of the Potomac to fight a defensive battle in its own territory. Time and again, Lee had beaten the Army of the Potomac, under a variety of commanders, in his home state of Virginia (most recently at the battle of Chancellorsville), with no discernable shift in the existing balance of power. A prolonged war favored the resource-rich North, and every soldier the South lost was difficult to replace.

Lincoln saw Lee's bold move not as a threat, but as an opportunity. He wrote to Joseph Hooker, then in command of the Army of the Potomac: "I think *Lee's army*, and not *Richmond*, is your true objective point," in response to Hooker's suggestion that he move into the vacuum left by Lee's departure and take the Confederate capital. Lincoln understood, as so many Union generals had yet to grasp, that as long as Lee's army was in the field, the rebellion was alive and well.

In that vein, he ordered Hooker to follow Lee, flank him, get in front of him, and force a battle. Hooker made excuses about why he needed more time, more troops, and more equipment, before he pursued Lee (in much the same manner as George B. McClellan had before him, as discussed in number 78). Lincoln recognized his hesitation as the reluctance of a commander who had lost once (and convincingly) to Lee at Chancellorsville, and was loath to do so again. Thus, when Hooker offered to resign over a technicality in his orders, Lincoln accepted. He replaced Hooker with one of the Army of the Potomac's corps commanders: George G. Meade.

Meade intended to intercept Lee in the vicinity of Cashtown, Pennsylvania. Instead, his cavalry bumped into Confederate skirmishers looking for shoes in the village of Gettysburg. Within three days, more than 150,000 men would come to blows on that spot. The climactic battle of the American Civil War had begun.

For once, Union forces had the luxury of fighting a defensive battle with superb interior lines of communication. The Confederates were unaccustomed to taking the offensive and trying to uproot their enemies from easily defended high ground. Coupled with this tactical advantage, George Meade and his army also benefited from Lee's overconfidence in his troops' superiority, and from the absence of Lee's cavalry. For two days, the Army of the Potomac held its ground.

On the third day, July 3, 1863, Lee foolishly ordered 13,000 men under General George Pickett to make a frontal assault on the Union center, entrenched on the heights at Cemetery Ridge. The Union Second Corps, under the command of General Winfield Scott Hancock, easily repulsed "Pickett's Charge"; his artillery and riflemen inflicted devastating casualties. After three days of bloody fighting, Lee withdrew, chastened by a casualty list numbering over 24,000 men.

Hungering for a decisive follow-up to Meade's victory at Gettysburg, Lincoln insisted his new commander follow Lee and attack him before he once again slipped across the Potomac and into Virginia. Having taken command less than a week before, and unsure of what sort of shape Lee's army was in, Meade was cautious in his pursuit. Lincoln urged General-in-Chief Henry W. Halleck to order Meade forward with all haste. Halleck responded by directing Meade to "push forward, and fight Lee before he can cross the Potomac."

But Meade failed to follow up on his advantage, and the Confederates crossed back into Virginia all but unmolested. Lincoln was beside himself. Secretary of the Navy Gideon V. Welles noted Lincoln's depression, writing, "On only one or two occasions have I ever seen the President so troubled, so dejected and discouraged." Because he couldn't very well fire a general who had been only recently promoted and had won such an overwhelming victory, Lincoln vented his displeasure in a letter he eventually chose not to send. He wrote: "I do not believe you appreciate the magnitude of the misfortune involved in Lee's escape. He was within your easy grasp, and to have closed upon him would, in connection with our other late successes, have ended the war. As it is, the war will be prolonged indefinitely." Meade was a fine battlefield commander, but he was understandably cautious, especially in light of his own army's casualties. Lincoln quickly realized he needed a commander willing to take the sorts of chances in the field that had won Lee his spectacular reputation over the previous two years.

On the same day as Pickett's Charge, the man Lincoln was looking for made his presence known by securing the entire Mississippi River for the Union. In the West, Ulysses S. Grant received the surrender of the Confederate garrison at Vicksburg.

84 Vicksburg: Lincoln finds his man

For more than one year, a Union army under Ulysses S. Grant's command had attempted to take the last Confederate stronghold on the Mississippi River: Vicksburg, Mississippi. Beginning in mid-1862, Grant's troops battled logistical problems and geography just to get into position to assault the fortress city. Swamps to the north and to the west impeded their progress, and the city's position on a bluff 200 feet above the Mississippi made it all but impossible for Union gunboats to run south under the guns of Vicksburg's garrison. Since the only truly practical thing to do was to take the city from the south, Grant spent months getting into position to besiege Vicksburg. By spring of 1863, his troops in the Union Army of the Tennessee were in position to do precisely that.

A regular army castoff forced to resign his commission because of rumors of excessive drunkenness and dereliction of duty during the 1850s, Grant had failed as both a farmer and a merchant. Working as a clerk in a family store in the Midwest when the war broke out, Grant immediately volunteered for service in the Illinois State Militia. Because of his prior military experience (he had served with distinction in the Mexican War), Grant began the war as a lieutenant colonel of Illinois volunteers.

He rose rapidly in rank afterward. Grant might have been a failure at everything and a lousy peacetime soldier (his lack of military bearing, in particular his indifference to the proper maintenance of his general's uniform, was legendary), but he proved himself a resourceful and adaptable battlefield commander. He won a near-bloodless victory at Fort Donelson on the Tennessee River, followed by an instructive near-defeat at Shiloh. By mid-1863, his star was on the rise.

Taking Vicksburg on July 4, 1863, was the coup that propelled Grant into the national limelight. In a brilliant campaign that cost him fewer than 10,000 total casualties, Grant inflicted at least an equal number of casualties on Confederate general John C. Pemberton's fortress garrison, in addition to taking nearly 30,000 prisoners and capturing 60,000 rifles and 172 artillery pieces.

Coming as it did on the heels of Meade's smashing victory at Getttysburg the previous day, the result at Vicksburg had two long-term effects. In the first place, it turned the Mississippi River into a Union highway, helping to tighten the bonds the Union's Anaconda Plan called for. Second, it convinced Abraham Lincoln that he had at last found a field commander daring, inventive, and bold enough to match Lee and wrest ultimate victory from him on the battlefield. Lincoln wasted little time in summoning Grant eastward and into a warm working and personal relationship that lasted until Lincoln's death in April of 1865. "Grant is my man," the president said, "and I am his the rest of the war."

85 The man invited as an afterthought: Abraham Lincoln at Gettysburg

"I should be glad, if I could flatter myself that I came as near to the central idea of the occasion, in two hours, as you did in two minutes."

—Edward Everett in a letter to Abraham Lincoln, November 19, 1863

"The cheek of every American must tingle with shame as he reads the silly, flat, and dishwatery utterances of the man who has to be pointed out to intelligent foreigners as the President of the United States."

—*The Chicago Times*, November 20, 1863

The Gettysburg Address is the most readily recognized speech in American history. It's also the most famous speech ever given by an American. At 284 words long, it has been called the perfect speech. And to think, it was offered for public consumption not as a featured speech, but as the epilogue to a two-hour presentation given by a retired president of Harvard.

In fact, inviting President Lincoln to even attend the dedication of the Gettysburg National Cemetery on November 19, 1863, was an afterthought on the part of the committee organizing the event. Expressing concern "as to [Lincoln's] ability to speak on such a grave and solemn occasion," the organizing committee wrote to the president to ask him to give the closing statement. Edward Everett, a former senator, congressman, governor of Massachusetts, ambassador to England, secretary of state, and president of Harvard College, gave the featured speech. Everett was one of the most admired public speakers in an age where public speakers had rock-star status. In nineteenth-century America people attended lectures much the same as we attend movies in the theaters today. People thought nothing of sitting through hours of oratory at a stretch, and Everett was a very popular public speaker, so any event where he "headlined" was a much-anticipated event.

This was the tough act that Lincoln was expected to follow. In the words of the invitation he received from the committee: "It is the desire that after the oration, you, as Chief Executive of the nation, formally set apart these grounds to their sacred use by a few appropriate remarks." Lincoln exceeded all expectations.

Myth has it that Lincoln jotted his speech down on the back of an envelope during part of the train ride from Washington, D.C. Nothing could be further from the truth. Lincoln spent weeks on his speech, wanting to make the most of the opportunity the event afforded.

At first it seemed he had missed his chance. Everett gave a spellbinding two-hour speech, ending with a rousing summation of the battle's importance and the combatants' timeless heroism. When he was done, he received thunderous applause from those assembled.

There was a photographer present, and when Everett finished, he set about switching the lenses in his camera. By the time he had finished (it only took a few minutes), Lincoln had already delivered his speech and sat back down again. Perhaps surprised by the brevity of the president's speech, the crowd gave a tepid response. When he sat, Lincoln told his friend and bodyguard Ward Lamon: "Lamon, that speech won't *scour*. It is a flat failure and the people are disappointed."

Only after the speech was published throughout the North did Lincoln begin to get a sense of how he had successfully tapped into the American psyche. His words were so potent, they helped him to redefine not only the nation's purpose in fighting for its survival, but also the very essence of the nation itself.

86 Did a sniper try to kill Lincoln in August 1864?

One night in August of 1864, our sixteenth president did something that may seem inconceivable to the modern reader. The chief executive of the United States rode away from the White House unescorted, on an old horse, headed in the direction of Soldier's Home, an establishment to which he frequently retreated to beat the dreadful Washington heat.

At some point not too far from Soldier's Home, Lincoln heard what sounded like a gunshot, and "Old Abe," as Lincoln's friend Ward Lamon was wont to call his horse, bolted. It took all of Lincoln's skill as a horseman to keep his seat. As it was, he lost his stovepipe hat. Lincoln apparently wasn't far from his destination, and within a couple of minutes he had arrived there safely, if a bit awry, in the saddle. Lincoln downplayed the incident, joking about it repeatedly, even after one of the sentries from Soldier's Home found the president's lost hat with a fresh bullet hole in it.

Lincoln privately expressed astonishment that anyone would want to kill him and humorously speculated that he had merely been the victim of some hunter carelessly discharging his loaded rifle. He steadfastly refused to discuss the possibility that he had been the victim of what would have been the first assassination attempt on a U.S. president.

On the other hand, he never again went to Soldier's Home unescorted. In fact, from August of 1864 on, Lincoln always rode to the presidential summer retreat in a carriage, accompanied by a fully armed escort of soldiers.

87 A strange twist of fate: The night John Wilkes Booth's brother saved Lincoln's son

The names Lincoln and Booth are inextricably linked in the minds of anyone who's ever studied American history. However, when John Wilkes Booth murdered President Abraham Lincoln in April of 1865, it was not the first time a Lincoln and a Booth had been in the same vicinity while a human life hung in the balance.

One of ten children, John Wilkes Booth was the son of the great Shakespearean actor Junius Brutus Booth. His brother Edwin Booth won mass acclaim as a Shakespearean actor (on both sides of the Atlantic) before his death in 1893.

The two brothers differed in a variety of ways. John Wilkes Booth was an ardent Southern sympathizer, but his brother Edwin supported the Northern cause and admired Lincoln. Edwin and John Wilkes were both so passionate in their politics that they frequently quarreled at family gatherings, culminating in Edwin asking his brother why he didn't enlist in the Confederate army, if he felt as strongly as he did. Wilkes (as he was called by family members) responded he had promised their mother he would remain out of the fighting. Edwin then insisted that politics never again be discussed at family gatherings.

In New York, Edwin Booth earned such acclaim he came to be remembered as the greatest Shakespearean actor of his time. During one stretch from 1863 to 1864, Edwin Booth played Hamlet in 100 consecutive performances.

He played to packed houses and rave reviews, channeling the pain he felt over the death of his wife earlier that year, and the shame he felt over being too drunk to respond when called to her deathbed, into a role that required oceans of both pain and shame. (He never again touched a drop of liquor.)

Because he traveled extensively when his company toured, Edwin Booth happened to be in Jersey City, waiting to board a southbound sleeper train in either 1863 or 1864 (the date is uncertain), when a young man was pushed by the press of the crowd, and slipped off the platform. He slid down between the trestle and the car he had been attempting to board. Nearly fifty years later he recalled the incident:

> *I was twisted off my feet, and had dropped somewhat, with feet downward, into the open space, and was personally helpless, when my coat collar was vigorously seized and I was quickly pulled up and out to a secure footing on the platform. Upon turning to thank my rescuer I saw it was Edwin Booth, whose face was of course well known to me, and I expressed my gratitude to him, and in doing so, called him by name.*

The young man's name was Robert Todd Lincoln. He was traveling from school in New York to visit his parents in Washington. The younger Lincoln remained convinced forever afterward that he would have died that night in Jersey City if not for Edwin Booth's intervention.

Edwin Booth went on to lose everything in bankruptcy during the 1870s. He rebuilt his fortune during the 1880s, and founded the Players' Club in New York. He died there in 1893, leaving his home as a headquarters for the club he had founded.

Robert Todd Lincoln was the only one of Lincoln's four children (all sons) to survive to adulthood. He became a successful Chicago attorney and served as secretary of war during the administrations of presidents Garfield and Arthur, and as ambassador to Great Britain for President Benjamin Harrison. After retiring from public life, Lincoln became president of the Pullman Car Company. He died in 1926.

Whether or not the two men ever spoke again is unrecorded. Edwin Booth was so distraught over his brother's murder of President Lincoln that he retired from the stage for nearly two years. He also never mentioned saving Lincoln's son's life shortly before.

88 "A Very Nearly Run Thing"?: The election of 1864

Once the question was asked whether a Democratic victory in the election of 1864 could result in a negotiated independence for the Confederacy, the Democrats were in serious trouble. To make matters worse, William T. Sherman's march through Georgia had effectively cut the Confederacy into three parts, and when Sherman took Atlanta shortly before the election, Lincoln's victory over his opponent, General George B. McClellan, seemed assured.

It had not always seemed such a sure shot. For one thing, no other country in recorded history had held elections (or would until World War II) during wartime, let alone during a *civil* war. Yet the idea of postponing the election until after ultimate victory never seems to have occurred to anyone in a position to suggest it. Lincoln was no exception. He said of the question: "We can not have free government without elections; and if the rebellion could force us to forego, or postpone a national election it might fairly claim to have already conquered and ruined us." Once he had been re-elected, Lincoln went on to point out that his re-election had shown that "a people's government can sustain a national election in the midst of a great civil war."

Even more remarkable, the national government allowed soldiers then in service to vote in an election that could alter their status as combatants. No other government had ever allowed this (including previous incarnations of the United States government). Nineteen states allowed their soldiers in the field to have their votes tallied, some of them separately, others mixed in with those of the civilians back home.

Surprisingly (or not surprisingly, depending on how you look at it), it was Democrats in states such as Indiana and Illinois who blocked the possibility of extending absentee ballots to troops in the field. The Democrats were running McClellan for president, and he was immensely popular among the common soldiers. His concern for their welfare was no secret.

As it turns out, the Democrats had good reason to fear the soldiers' vote. Because they seem to have felt that too many had suffered to acquiesce to a negotiated peace at the hands of a Democratic administration, the armed services voted overwhelmingly for Lincoln. As one soldier put it, "We all want peace, but none any but an *honorable* one. I had rather stay out here a lifetime (much as I dislike it) than consent to a division of our country." In all fairness to McClellan, he insisted on continuing the war and defeating the Confederacy on the battlefield. However, in so doing, he differed with the Democratic Party leadership, which was no secret.

By the time of the election, Lincoln had a commanding lead in the polls. He crushed McClellan in one of the most lopsided electoral victories ever: Lincoln had 212 electoral votes to McClellan's twenty-one. McClellan carried only Delaware, Kentucky, and New Jersey (where he was later elected governor and served two terms shortly before his death in 1885). Lincoln, the nation, and by extension, the concept of representative democracy, had won.

"The better angels of our nature": The Second Inaugural Address

89

> "Both parties deprecated war; but one of them would *make* war rather than let the nation survive; and the other would *accept* war rather than let it perish. And the war came."

—Abraham Lincoln in his Second Inaugural Address, March 4, 1865

March 4, 1865, arrived in the national capital cold, wet, and dreary. Because most Washington streets were unpaved, people slogged through a sea of mud to watch Abraham Lincoln take his second oath of office as the president of the United States. His amazing speech at Gettysburg notwithstanding, many people had yet to discover the depth of Lincoln's ability to frame a complex issue simply and succinctly. Still others knew well his deserved reputation as an orator. These people expected Lincoln would use the occasion of his second inaugural ceremony to address the anticipated end of the war and how he would treat the defeated Southern states. He did not disappoint them.

They did, however, have to wait through the new vice president's inauguration ceremony, which took place in the Senate chamber. Andrew Johnson, a War Democrat and former senator from Tennessee, was added the previous November to the ticket to bolster Lincoln's electoral support in border states like Kentucky, West Virginia, and Maryland. Poorly educated (he had been a tinker before entering politics), inarticulate, and terribly ill-tempered, Johnson made his inauguration interesting by showing up for it dead drunk. In a rambling speech, he condemned the rich and the powerful ("with all your fine feathers and gewgaws"), pointing out that they owed their wealth and positions to the common people. Lincoln sat silently through Johnson's speech, and when the new vice president had finished, he quietly told the parade marshal, "Do not let Johnson speak outside."

Next the inaugural party moved outdoors, in front of the Capitol, where former Treasury Secretary (now Chief Justice of the U.S. Supreme Court) Salmon P. Chase swore in Lincoln and Lincoln gave his speech. And what a speech it was! In just over 700 words, Lincoln reiterated the reasons both sides went to war, summarized the sacrifices made to preserve the nation as a whole, and clarified his position on how the nation should proceed once the last shot had been fired. In a moment made for television, Lincoln stepped to the podium to give his speech, and the rain stopped. Then, in his high-pitched voice, Abraham Lincoln delivered the last great speech of his life.

He invoked God. He mentioned the Bible. He promised to take any measure that would not just preserve the Union but eradicate slavery, even if, as he said, "God wills that [the war] continue, until all the wealth piled by the bond-man's two hundred and fifty years of unrequited toil shall be sunk, and until every drop of blood drawn with the lash, shall be paid by another drawn with the sword."

As with all of his great speeches, Lincoln's Second Inaugural Address concluded on an inspirational, invocatory note:

With malice toward none; with charity for all; with firmness in the right, as God gives us to see the right, let us strive on to finish the work we are in; to bind up the nation's wounds; to care for him who shall have borne the battle, and for his widow, and his orphan—to do all which may achieve and cherish a just, and a lasting peace, among ourselves, and with all nations.

Lincoln made a point of not differentiating between Northern and Southern veterans or their widows or orphans in calling on the nation to help heal the wounds inflicted by the devastating war. Despite the loud protests of Radical Republicans in Congress, he wanted to be lenient with the returning Southern states. He enunciated this desire shortly before his death, when he said that his main concern in concluding the war was "to get the men composing the Confederate armies back to their homes, at work on their farms or in their shops."

It is entirely possible that Lincoln might have succeeded in carrying out his reconstruction program of the Southern states, had he lived much past the end of the war. As it happened, Lincoln was dead within weeks of Lee's final surrender at Appomattox Courthouse in April 1865, and his successor, Andrew Johnson, although disposed by his Tennessee roots to deal lightly with the South, did not possess the requisite political skills to do so while also handling the Republican Congress. The result was not Lincoln's hoped-for quick recovery from four years of bloody civil war, but military occupation, a power struggle in the highest reaches of the federal government, and the eventual first impeachment of a sitting president of the United States. All of these things probably wouldn't have happened had Abraham Lincoln lived to serve out the second term that began so promisingly on that rainy March day when the sun unexpectedly came out at just the right moment.

90 Ultimate victory: Appomattox, April 1865

"The war is over. The rebels are our countrymen again."

—Union general Ulysses S. Grant, April 9, 1865

Early in the afternoon of April 9, 1865, Confederate general Robert E. Lee surrendered what was left of the Army of Northern Virginia to Ulysses S. Grant, commanding general of the Union armies. Lee's army, which at one time numbered more than 70,000 men, had shrunk to just 12,500 men. Ragged, exhausted, and hungry, the rebels had led Grant's men on a long chase during their retreat westward from Richmond when Lee had evacuated the Confederacy's capital city a week earlier. There were smaller armies still at large in North Carolina and out in the Western theater, but with Lee's surrender, Southern resistance had been all but extinguished. The Civil War was over.

Upon receiving the telegram Grant sent relating Lee's surrender on April 10, Lincoln was elated, but he did not make any immediate public comment.

When a large crowd returned to the White House lawn the following evening, the president addressed them from a window. His manner was grave, his expression thoughtful. He waited a long time for silence before addressing those assembled. If they expected a victory speech, they were disappointed. Lincoln was already looking toward the future, trying to come up with a plan for healing a nation torn almost asunder by four years of terrible civil war. At length, he spoke: "Fellow citizens," he began, "We are met this evening not in sorrow, but in gladness of heart. The evacuation of Petersburg and Richmond, and the surrender of the principal insurgent army, give hope of a righteous and speedy peace whose joyous expression cannot be restrained."

After waiting a moment for the resultant cheers to die down, he continued:

By these recent successes, the re-inauguration of the national authority—reconstruction—which has had a large share of thought from the first, is pressed much more closely upon our attention. It is fraught with great difficulty. Unlike the case of a war between independent nations, there is no authorized organ for us to treat with—no one man has authority to give up the rebellion for any other man. We simply must begin with, and mold from, organized and discordant elements. Nor is it a small additional embarrassment that we, the loyal people, differ among ourselves as to the mode, manner, and means of reconstruction.

Even in this, what might have easily been considered Lincoln's moment of well-deserved triumph, our sixteenth president took no time for self-congratulatory talk. Instead, Lincoln, ever the master politician and now a mature and clear-eyed statesman, used the moment to begin the next difficult task before him. He wanted to hammer out a reconstruction program that allowed for a speedy reconciliation of the opposing sides, so the country could truly begin to heal. This action, as much as anything else he did during his four-plus years as chief executive, speaks loudly to both the greatness of Abraham Lincoln and his evolution from brilliant trial lawyer and wily politician into a genuine leader for his people. When viewed from this perspective, his murder, just weeks after the end of general hostilities between the North and the South, seems all the more tragic. How much bitterness and needless suffering could the nation have avoided had Lincoln been alive to lend his enormous political prestige to the reconstruction cause? How might his influence have calmed the stormy seas of the political process during the latter part of the 1860s?

We will never know for sure. One thing is certain, though. He couldn't have botched the job any worse than Andrew Johnson, the man who replaced him as president.

91 Ultimate defeat: Ford's Theatre, April 1865

"Creswell, old fellow, everything is bright this morning. The war is over. It has been a tough time, but we have lived it out. Or some of us have. But it is over. We are going to have good times now, and a united country."

—Abraham Lincoln, to Maryland senator John Creswell,
on the morning of the day he died

At just after 10 P.M. on the night of April 14, 1865, President Abraham Lincoln was enjoying a performance of a hackneyed farce known as *Our American Cousin* in the presidential box at Ford's Theatre, in Washington, D.C. Leaning forward in the rocking chair from which he usually enjoyed theatrical productions, Lincoln was intent on the stage below him, when actor John Wilkes Booth, the alcoholic, egomaniacal brother of America's greatest tragic actor, slipped into the presidential box and shot the president behind his left ear. Lincoln slumped forward, unconscious. Booth struggled briefly with Major Henry Rathbone, one of Lincoln's guests in the presidential box that evening, wounding Rathbone in the arm with the hunting knife he carried.

Then jumping to the stage (in doing so he broke his left leg), Booth, an actor to the end, melodramatically raised his bloody knife over his head and reportedly recited the Virginia state motto *"Sic Semper Tyrannis"* ("Thus always to tyrants") before limping offstage and out the back door, where he had a horse waiting.

Booth's attack on Lincoln was part of a wider conspiracy to kill the president, Vice President Andrew Johnson, and Secretary of State William H. Seward, all on the same night. The conspirator detailed to kill the vice president lost his nerve and went off to get drunk instead. Lewis Powell, a Texan who also went by the last name of Paine, did succeed in attacking Seward in his home, but Seward resisted, and escaped with superficial knife wounds.

Within a week, Booth had been run aground and shot to death when he refused to surrender to pursuing Union troops. All but one of his coconspirators had been apprehended and imprisoned, and were pending trial. The fanatically pro-Southern Booth had tried to kidnap Lincoln the previous year, with the idea of taking Lincoln to Richmond and ransoming captured Confederate troops in return for the president's safe return. That scheme backfired because Lincoln's plans changed at the last moment. Wilkes Booth had had an opportunity to meet Lincoln a couple of years previously, when the president had attended one of his performances. Lincoln had been so impressed with the young actor's ability he had sent a note backstage requesting the opportunity to meet Booth, but Booth coolly and politely declined. Is it possible that Booth later regretted not taking the opportunity to get close enough to the president to kill him?

Ironically, Lincoln had initially intended to forgo the theater on the evening of Booth's attack. In the end, he decided to go to the theater because word got out that he and Mrs. Lincoln would be there, and he did not want to disappoint the public. "It has been advertised that we will be there," Lincoln said, "and I cannot disappoint the people. Otherwise I would not go. I do not want to go."

Mortally wounded, Lincoln was carried across the street to a house owned by a Swedish tailor. He died just after 7 A.M. the following morning, without regaining consciousness. Upon his being pronounced dead, War Secretary Edwin M. Stanton stood at the foot of the bed on which Lincoln's body lay, removed his hat in salute, and said, "Now he belongs to the ages."

And so he does.

Part 5

Comparisons and Contemporaries

How does the life of Abraham Lincoln compare to those of other great statesmen? Lincoln and Jefferson Davis were born less than a year apart, within 100 miles of each other, in frontier Kentucky. Were their lives similar or different? How does Lincoln stack up as a chief executive against giants such as Washington and Jefferson? The details are certainly intriguing.

92 Lincoln and Washington

George Washington and Abraham Lincoln: one set precedents about how the executive branch of the American republic wields power; the other broke many of these aforementioned precedents to safeguard this same American republic. On the surface, these two men seem to have little in common. Yet their names are inextricably linked, and they invariably come up when conversation turns to leadership in a republic.

Washington was born into a well-to-do land-owning family in Virginia. His father died when he was a boy, and young George endured a strained relationship with his demanding mother. His elder brother, Lawrence, inherited all of their father's holdings, as was customary at the time. Lawrence then helped to set George up in business as a surveyor and gentleman farmer.

Lincoln's birth was far humbler than Washington's. He was born in Kentucky, a poor farmer's son. His situation with his parents was the reverse of Washington's: He lost his mother early, and had a strained relationship with his father for decades. Lincoln had no elder brother to set him up in business, although he did teach himself how to survey, and made his principal living in that manner for a number of years in the mid-1830s.

Washington made his reputation in the military, and saw extensive action on the Ohio frontier during the so-called French and Indian War (1754–61). Lincoln had brief experience as a militiaman on the Illinois frontier in the Black Hawk War of 1832, but saw no action. Both men served for long periods in their local governments (Washington in Virginia's House of Burgesses, and Lincoln in the Illinois State Legislature), and they enjoyed enormous prestige among their colleagues.

Both men married late in life (for their respective times), and both married daughters of wealthy Southern slave-owning families. Washington (who was likely sterile) married an extremely wealthy widow with children from her first marriage, and sired no children of his own. Lincoln did not own slaves and did not directly profit monetarily from his marriage to Mary Todd (although she did bear him four children). Although Washington did own slaves, he treated them very well, avoided selling any of them, and freed them in his will (the only slave-owning Founding Father to do so).

Both men were abnormally tall for their time, and were the same height (6'4"). In Washington's case, this combined with his natural reserve, made him an even more commanding figure. In Lincoln's case, with his careless dress and outgoing manner, the height merely lent to the general perception of him as a physical oddity. While Washington was not as intellectually astute as Lincoln, he was possibly as shrewd a judge of character. Both men had slow-working, methodical minds, and both were successful in their private business endeavors.

After the end of the Revolution, Washington (still in command of the Continental army) refused to seize power from the Continental Congress, even though some of his officers encouraged him to do so. What's more, Washington had a limited view of the president's—and the entire executive branch's—role. He acted upon that view, setting a number of precedents that helped to place certain limits on presidential power, on which the U.S. Constitution (Washington presided over the convention that drafted and ratified it) was mute. In so doing, Washington was ably assisted by such trusted members of his cabinet as Secretary of the Treasury Alexander Hamilton and Secretary of State Thomas Jefferson.

Lincoln did not have the luxury of practicing restraint once he took office. He was dealing with a nation embroiled in a bitter civil war and a capital city in the heart of the slave belt, in danger of being isolated by further secession. And, as payment for the political deals he'd struck at the 1860 Republican National Convention in Chicago, he had agreed to fill his cabinet with political rivals, the foremost of whom, Secretary of State William H. Seward and Secretary of the Treasury Salmon P. Chase, despised each other. Jefferson and Hamilton had disagreed strongly as well, and had competed for Washington's opinion on matters of state, to the point where Jefferson resigned. Though Chase and Seward did not share Jefferson and Hamilton's affection for their chief executive (in Seward's case this changed after he had spent time in Lincoln's cabinet), they did squabble over Lincoln's direction for the country.

Lincoln jailed pro-Confederate leaders without trial, suspending the writ of habeas corpus (the right to a speedy trial), something Washington would have found unforgivable. He also struggled (at least at first) to win his party's nomination for re-election in the 1864 campaign. Washington won his in a walk. Washington enjoyed the honorific title "Father of His Country" during his lifetime, and his personal prestige infused the presidency with more intrinsic legitimacy at the time when it needed it most. Not so Lincoln. He was the butt of ridicule for most of his presidency. It was only in death that he became a martyr on a scale that eventually eclipsed that of Washington.

 ## 93 Lincoln and Jefferson

One was "the Sage of Monticello," a true polymath, a last Renaissance man whose range of accomplishments was as varied as it was astounding. The other was "the Great Emancipator," carrying forward to its natural conclusion the work the Sage had begun a mere "four-score and seven years" before. They were, of course, Thomas Jefferson and Abraham Lincoln, and together they represented the beginning and the end of the antislavery movement in U.S. history.

Jefferson was the Great Sphinx of American history. An Enlightenment thinker who questioned the validity of slavery, he wrote the immortal words "All men are created equal" in the American Declaration of Independence, a revolutionary sentiment for a revolutionary document. Lincoln issued the Emancipation Proclamation, which helped to bring about the end of slavery in the United States by 1865.

As was the case with Lincoln, Jefferson was tough to pin down on the practice of slavery itself. Although he decried the evils of slavery in his writing, he owned hundreds of slaves himself (including, apparently, a slave mistress who bore him several children). And unlike George Washington, Jefferson did not free all of his slaves, even upon his death. (This was in part because of the crushing debt he had inherited from his father-in-law, John Randolph. Jefferson struggled with the debt for the remainder of his own life.)

For his part, Lincoln never owned slaves, and often said, "If slavery isn't a sin, nothing is." But he avoided abolitionists for most of his political career because of his distaste for zealotry. Because of that distaste, Lincoln never bothered to join an established church. Like Jefferson (who was a deist and believed in an inactive "clock-maker" God, who set the universe in motion, then sat back and watched things unfold), he was denounced in certain quarters as an atheist.

Where Jefferson was born into a wealthy family of Virginia planters, Lincoln was born to poor, illiterate sharecroppers. Both men lost parents when they were young (Jefferson both parents, and Lincoln his mother). Jefferson married young, and lost his wife while still in his thirties. He promised her on her deathbed that he would never remarry, and he kept his word. Lincoln married later in life, and his wife survived him. Both men knew the deep sadness of having several of their own children predecease them. In fact, both men had only one of several offspring live past childhood. In Jefferson's case it was his eldest daughter, and in Lincoln's case, his eldest son.

Both men had their problems with the opposition and the country itself when they occupied the White House. Jefferson embarked on a disastrous economic plan that called for an embargo on European trade goods for as long as the European powers (deeply embroiled in the Napoleonic Wars at the time) refused to recognize American neutrality. This protectionist policy nearly wrecked the fledgling national economy and proved that although Jefferson might have been a first-rate linguist/historian/philosopher/engineer, he had no head for economics.

Where Jefferson was really the author of most of his own misfortunes during his administration, Lincoln had most of his thrust upon him because of the Civil War. Jefferson earned the goodwill of the people for having been the author of the Declaration of Independence and for serving as governor of Virginia, U.S. secretary of state, and vice president. Lincoln had several tours in the Illinois State Legislature and one two-year term in the U.S. House of Representatives under his belt when he won the presidency. So, although his unsuccessful run for the U.S. Senate in 1858 made him a nationally recognized political figure, his record in national politics was far spottier than Jefferson's.

Finally, it is interesting to note that Jefferson had great respect for the U.S. Supreme Court's decisions, whereas Lincoln had little. Jefferson made a point of abiding by such landmark Supreme Court decisions as *Marbury* v. *Madison*, which helped establish the precedent of judicial review. But Lincoln suspended the writ of habeas corpus and indefinitely jailed several pro-Confederate political leaders in Maryland because he was worried about Maryland possibly seceding from the Union. Supreme Court Chief Justice Roger B. Taney ruled against Lincoln in *Ex Parte Merryman*, and ordered that all jailed Southern-sympathizing political leaders in Maryland be freed. Lincoln ignored his order, justifiably citing reasons of national security.

Ironic, indeed, in light of both men's views on the question of liberty, and the lengths to which one of them (the one who actually jailed American citizens without trial) went to secure it for all citizens in the long run.

94 Lincoln and Jackson

Any comparison of "Old Hickory" Andrew Jackson and Abraham Lincoln is filled with both stark contrasts and interesting similarities. Jackson was president when Lincoln entered active politics at the state level in the 1830s. Lincoln, a lifelong admirer of Jackson's eternal political foe Henry Clay, was (in his own words) "always a Whig" (the opposing political party that formed around Clay once Jackson was president), and thus by association a foe of Jackson's Democrats.

However, the two men had many things in common. Jackson was the first man to win the presidency with anything like a mandate from the common man (whose interests he insisted he best represented). And, although born in South Carolina, he was as much a product of the frontier as Lincoln himself.

Like Lincoln, Jackson learned the political process courtesy of the frontier political institution's rough-hewn backwoods system. Unlike Lincoln, Jackson had a violent temper. Also unlike Lincoln, Jackson rose rapidly through the ranks of political patronage. Jackson studied law (as Lincoln did) by "reading the law" in the office of an established attorney, and then began to practice law. The two men shared a courtroom reputation for success, although for different reasons. Lincoln's forte was winning over a jury by making them like and trust him, then leading them with inescapable logic to his desired conclusion. Jackson was a fiery orator who moved men with his passion and his almost indomitable will.

Jackson quickly became a frontier judge; then he was the first man from Tennessee elected to the U.S. House of Representatives. Afterward, he spent a brief amount of time as a U.S. senator. Lincoln, who was never more than a "fill-in" magistrate, served several terms in the Illinois State Legislature, and only one term as a U.S. congressman. He did run for the U.S. Senate twice, and lost both times.

The two men most differed professionally in their military careers. As a boy, Jackson was captured and terribly wounded while serving in the American Revolution. He was a general of Tennessee militia for decades, commanding troops during the War of 1812 and in a series of wars against the Creek Confederacy in northern Alabama and Mississippi. Lincoln was briefly an officer of Illinois militia during the Black Hawk War of 1832, but never saw any action, and later counted himself lucky for not having needed to fire a shot in anger. Also, Jackson's fierce temper led him to duel with (and kill) a man who had made disparaging comments about his beloved wife, Rachel, and while Lincoln himself never fought a duel over his wife, he came close (see number 25).

Oddly enough, Jackson and Lincoln shared a number of similar traits as chief executive. Like Lincoln, Jackson had little respect for the U.S. Supreme Court and refused to enforce several of its rulings. Also like Lincoln, Jackson had to deal with his cabinet's incredible insubordination, in the form of Vice President John C. Calhoun. Up until 1832, Calhoun was Jackson's handpicked successor. But Calhoun ghostwrote a position paper claiming that the individual states could nullify laws passed by the national government (a position Jackson vigorously opposed). Calhoun's home state of South Carolina, which depended overwhelmingly on foreign trade (think cotton), led the charge in the Nullification Crisis. South Carolina vowed that state militia troops would keep federal customs inspectors from collecting duties called for under the so-called Tariff of Abominations (passed in 1828), and Calhoun tacitly supported this position.

When Jackson got wind of this, he showed himself to be every bit the ardent Unionist that Abraham Lincoln showed himself to be a generation later. Publicly, he nationalized the South Carolina state armories and moved federal troops in to ensure the customs duties would be collected and rebellion among the common people would be avoided. Privately, he called in Calhoun and coldly promised him that if things got out of hand in South Carolina, Calhoun was the first man Jackson would hang as a traitor. You can only wonder what might have happened in December 1860 had James Buchanan moved so decisively. By the time Lincoln took office in 1861, it was too late for such pre-emptive action. The Civil War had begun in earnest.

95 Lincoln and Buchanan

"When I parted the Executive Mansion, I said to President Lincoln: 'If you are as happy, my dear sir, on entering this house as I am in leaving it and returning home, [then] you are the happiest man in this country.'"

—James Buchanan, March 1861

James Buchanan was Abraham Lincoln's immediate predecessor in the White House. His watch witnessed such momentous events as the Dred Scott decision, the passage of a proslavery Lecompton Constitution for the new state of Kansas, and the Lincoln-Douglas debates. Most tellingly, on December 20, 1860, with more than three months to go in Buchanan's term as president, South Carolina seceded from the Union.

Buchanan's responses to these occurrences were to support the ludicrous Dred Scott decision, support the Lecompton Constitution, and ignore the Lincoln-Douglas debates. Most importantly, when South Carolina seceded, Buchanan did . . . nothing.

Buchanan and Lincoln were very different men. Where Buchanan did not wish to be remembered for allowing a civil war to begin during his presidency, Lincoln accepted the necessity of fighting that war once the seceding South thrust it upon him. Where Buchanan sympathized with Southerners, and filled his cabinet with proslavery men (thereby alienating the Northern Democrats), Lincoln insisted that slavery would not be restricted where it was already in practice, but it could not be extended farther.

One thing these two men did have in common were tragic love affairs in their youths. Buchanan became engaged at age twenty-eight to a twenty-three-year-old Lancaster girl named Ann Coleman. Buchanan later broke off the engagement, and Coleman committed suicide shortly thereafter. Lincoln's first fiancée, Ann Rutledge, died in her early twenties and Lincoln was nearly prostrate with grief. Of the two, only Lincoln married. Buchanan spent his entire life a bachelor.

There can be little question that as a president, Lincoln was everything Buchanan was not: decisive, compassionate, and a strong leader. Buchanan, the ultimate and lifelong political insider, was completely unsuited to the role of president, and most especially unsuited to the task of presiding over a nation rapidly unraveling along sectional lines. Then again, it's possible that there was no man (or woman) ever born who could have turned the tide away from secession and civil war by the late 1850s. As it was, it took a great man to put back together what over "four score" years of sectional strife had finally torn asunder.

96 Lincoln and Clay

Abraham Lincoln became a Whig because he admired fellow Kentuckian Henry Clay. Aside from their Kentucky connection (Clay was born in Virginia, and Lincoln grew up mostly in Indiana and Illinois), the two men had little in common beyond certain cherished political views. Lincoln was at best a minor politician for much of his adult life, coming to true political prominence during the 1850s, in his mid-forties. By his mid-thirties, Henry Clay had already been elected a U.S. senator. He was also a U.S. congressman, in addition to serving a term as the Speaker of the Kentucky House of Representatives.

Clay was a career politician who served five different terms as a U.S. senator between 1806 and his death in 1852. He was also twice secretary of state and Speaker of the U.S. House of Representatives. He also ran for president three times, in 1824, 1832, and 1844. (He lost all three times.) After his last loss, he reportedly said, "I would rather be right than president." This is unlikely. Clay wanted to be president more than the IRS wants to know when you win the lottery.

Known as "the Great Compromiser," Clay was instrumental in the construction of three great compromises, which helped to ease sectional strife in antebellum America from 1820 through 1850. As Speaker of the House, Clay had a direct hand in drafting the Missouri Compromise, which settled (for a generation at least) the question of slavery in America's western territories. During the Nullification Crisis of the early 1830s, he came up with the Tariff

Compromise of 1833. And in 1850, less than two years before his death in 1852 at age seventy-four, he engineered his last great compromise, the Compromise of 1850, which helped to stave off civil war over the questions of states' rights and slavery.

Lincoln's political resume up until 1860 was not nearly as sterling as Clay's. Yet Lincoln succeeded where Clay failed: He won election to the presidency not once, but twice. Ultimately, Lincoln's legacy transcended Clay's because the consequences of his political agenda were longer lasting and he had greater long-term impact on the American people's lives.

Clay (who was as Unionist and antislavery as Lincoln) had only been able to buy time on the question of sectionalist strife, and he was never successfully able to address the question of slavery in America. (His attempts to get slavery outlawed in his home state of Kentucky were a flat failure.) But Lincoln settled both issues in less than four years.

One dubious distinction both men shared was posthumous participation in a political trend that Clay initiated. Henry Clay was the first American to be given a state funeral in the rotunda of the U.S. Capitol building (upon his death in 1852). Lincoln was given one thirteen years later. In death, these two men had more in common than they ever had in life.

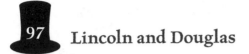

97 Lincoln and Douglas

If Abraham Lincoln had one great political nemesis throughout his life, it was Senator Stephen A. Douglas of Illinois. From Douglas's perspective this statement might have seemed backward. For Douglas, who rapidly climbed the political ladder of success throughout the 1830s, 1840s, and 1850s, Lincoln was the dangerous adversary, since Douglas had little to gain and everything to lose whenever the two butted heads.

When Lincoln wanted to debate Douglas as early as 1854 over slavery in U.S. territories where the Missouri Compromise had previously outlawed it in 1820, Douglas refused. Douglas once called Lincoln the most dangerous man he had ever met.

In many ways the two were physical opposites. Douglas was stoutly built, with a massive head and powerful torso placed on short, stovepipe legs. Lincoln was tall and so spare he looked nearly emaciated. Douglas had the rich, deep voice of a born orator, in an age where a three-hour speech was considered first-class entertainment. Lincoln had a high-pitched, nasal voice with a pronounced prairie twang.

Both Lincoln and Douglas were born in other states and migrated as young men to Illinois. Douglas was born in Vermont, grew up there and in New York, and then settled in Ohio for a time. Lincoln was born in Kentucky, raised there and in Indiana, and then moved to Illinois.

Douglas was trained as a carpenter before going to college. Lincoln's father was a carpenter (among other things), but Lincoln had no interest in following him into that profession. Douglas taught school in northern Illinois for a while. Lincoln, with less than one year of formal schooling under his belt, once termed his education "deficient." He was almost completely self-educated.

Interestingly, Douglas and Lincoln both courted Mary Todd (the future Mrs. Lincoln), and the differences in their respective natures made all the difference in the world when it came down to whom she would eventually marry. Douglas's courtship was halfhearted at best. He and Mary Todd both realized that their personalities were not truly compatible. Both sought the limelight, were outgoing, and loved to be the center of attention. While that made for highly entertaining repartee, it didn't necessarily make for a good marriage. Lincoln had better luck because the temperament that later drove his wife to distraction better suited her own high-strung nature. Regardless, Douglas and Mary Todd were friends of long acquaintance. In fact, he asked her for the first dance at her husband's inaugural ball.

These two men were most alike, yet they also (paradoxically) differed most in their opinion of slavery. Both Douglas and Lincoln were personally opposed to slavery. Where they truly differed was in how best to deal with it politically. As the political outsider seen as a rising star at the head of a new party, Lincoln had the luxury of being able to be vague on slavery. On the other hand, Douglas, at the head of the Democratic Party for most of the 1850s, had to stand on his own record. Where Lincoln said he was personally opposed to slavery, but would respect its legal right where it already existed, Douglas took a more accommodating approach. He tried to appease the Southerners in his party with such stratagems as the Kansas-Nebraska Act, which would have left it up to the populations of new states as to whether they would enter the Union as a slave state or as a free state. Douglas believed that this process, known as popular sovereignty, would appease Southerners sensitive to increasingly strident abolitionist calls for the end of slavery throughout the United States. He also believed that it was a largely empty gesture, because the unorganized territory's climate did not lend itself to growing labor-intensive cash crops such as cotton.

So Douglas stood on his record in 1858, when Lincoln challenged him for his U.S. Senate seat. He won largely because Illinois was still an overwhelmingly Democratic state, and at the time, state legislatures rather than voters, elected senators (this changed in 1913). Douglas again stood on his record two years later, when he ran (once more against Lincoln) for the U.S. presidency. By this time, Douglas had modified his stance on slavery, opposing the proslavery Kansas state constitution, called the Lecompton Constitution. This opposition cost him the support of the Southern wing of the Democratic Party, which bolted from the Democratic National Convention, reconvened as the Constitutional Union Party, and nominated its own candidate, John Bell.

With the Democratic Party shattered, Lincoln won the presidency in a landslide, and Douglas's political wheeling and dealing came to naught. Douglas lived just long enough to pledge his support for the new administration in its struggle to maintain the Union, then died at home in Chicago, in June, 1861.

98 Lincoln and Davis

Born in Kentucky, within 100 miles and one year of each other, these two men were transported geographically in different directions as children. Jefferson Davis was born on June 3, 1808, in Christian County (present-day Todd County), Kentucky. While he was still young, his Virginia-born father moved the family to northern Mississippi. Davis's father made a fortune raising cotton, and his son grew up in a prosperous Southern planter's household. Lincoln's own father was also born in Virginia, but lacking the support of a father who died prematurely in a 1784 Indian attack, he grew up to be an itinerant, barely literate laborer. He also moved the family across the Ohio River to western Indiana while his son was still young.

The difference in their circumstances growing up was evident in the educations the two men received. Lincoln had less than a single year of formal schooling (unsurprising for someone growing up in a poor frontier farm family), whereas Davis received local schooling in Mississippi before winning an appointment to the United States Military Academy at West Point. He graduated in 1828. Thus began Jefferson Davis's constant back-and-forth shuffle between military and public service.

Both men served during the Black Hawk War of 1832, Davis as an officer in the regular army, and Lincoln as a captain (and then as a private after re-enlisting once his initial obligation ran out) in the Illinois militia. Both men also loved and lost tragically during the mid-1830s. Lincoln's fiancée, Ann

Rutledge, died of a fever. Davis eloped in 1835 with Sarah Knox Taylor (General and future president Zachary Taylor's daughter), who died of an unknown illness, likely malaria, shortly after. Both men later married during the 1840s.

Both men were also elected to the U.S. House of Representatives in the 1840s. They never served together, though, because Davis resigned to fight in the Mexican War before Lincoln began to serve his single term (1847–49). Davis was wounded at the climactic battle of Buena Vista, returned home a hero, and won election to the U.S. Senate. By contrast, Lincoln finished his term, did not seek re-election (because of Whig precedent), went home to Springfield, and worked on building his law practice into one of the foremost in the state.

The 1850s saw Davis serving exclusively in national office, while Lincoln became a successful corporate attorney. Between 1850 and 1861, Davis was first in the Senate and then served in President Franklin Pierce's cabinet as his secretary of war. (After Pierce left office in 1857, Davis returned to the Senate.) Lincoln continued to try cases and charge fees while seeking a seat in the U.S. Senate in 1854, and again in 1858. Lincoln's election to the presidency in 1860 set in motion a series of events that culminated in Davis's resigning from his Senate post in January of 1861. Ultimately, he was selected as the first (and only) president of the Confederate States of America.

These two men were very different in their approaches to executive office. Davis, an ardent advocate of states' rights while a senator, found (as had Thomas Jefferson before him) that working with a legislature could be difficult for a chief executive without centralizing more authority than was called for by the Confederate constitution. Lincoln, too, had to deal with an at-times recalcitrant Congress. However, where Davis failed to get legislative cooperation much of the time, Lincoln, the affable, storytelling charmer, was usually able to get what he wanted.

Oddly enough, Davis's own patrician upbringing, which had afforded him so many advantages unknown to someone of Lincoln's humble origins, might have put him at a disadvantage. Many people with whom he attempted to work on the Confederate government saw him as aloof, aristocratic, and difficult. Chief among these was his own vice president, Alexander H. Stephens of Georgia. Ironically, Stephens had served in Congress with Lincoln, and the two became close political allies.

The long and the short of it is that a lifetime of trial and error before he took office in March of 1861 had taught Lincoln how to work well with all manner of people. Davis had less experience at attempting to compromise with people he did not consider his social equals. Their respective governments were greatly affected by both their temperaments.

Davis outlived Lincoln by twenty-four years, dying in New Orleans in 1889. During that time, he wrote a set of memoirs wherein he spent a lot of time pointing the finger elsewhere for the Confederacy's demise. It is inconceivable that Abraham Lincoln would have taken such a view if the roles were reversed. He felt the heavy burden of the responsibility he had shouldered along with the presidency. It showed in his face, in his mannerisms. As journalist David R. Locke later said of Lincoln: "His was the saddest face I ever looked upon."

Part 6

Lincoln and His Legacy

What is Abraham Lincoln's enduring legacy? What meaning can we take from the life this great man lived? Who can claim him? Who tries to? Why did someone attempt to steal Lincoln's body? There is little doubt that our sixteenth president has left a lasting impact on the nation and the effects of his leadership will continue to be felt for generations to come. Read on to learn more. . . .

99 A nation in mourning: Lincoln's immediate legacy

Lincoln's metamorphosis from embattled-if-able politician to secular saint began the moment that news of his murder started to spread. Almost overnight people who had voted for his political enemies, and those very political enemies themselves, began to change their stories and extol his virtues as politician, president, and improbable savior of the Union.

In Lincoln's own party, the radicals, who had opposed him at so many turns and had howled about his reluctance to free the slaves and for his willingness to deal gently with a defeated South at the end of the war, began to sing his praises—as did the Democrats, who had condemned him for freeing the slaves, and for not being conciliatory enough with the South when he first took office. The level of hypocrisy involved was almost laughable, even among politicians.

As far as Lincoln's immediate family was concerned, the blow of his death was understandably devastating. His wife, Mary, never the most stable of women, took to the widow's weeds immediately and stayed in the White House for almost two months after her husband's murder. When government officials were finally able to pry her out of the executive mansion, she took Lincoln's casket on an extended tour through a number of states. The long funeral ride eerily mirrored the long train ride Lincoln had taken to Washington, D.C., for his inauguration as president four years previously. In 1861, Lincoln had taken a circuitous route from his home in Illinois to the capital so the American people could get a glimpse of the man about whom they knew so little, and from whom they expected so much. In 1865, his funeral train took an equally roundabout route back to Springfield so that the American people, most of whom still knew so little about him, could have a chance to properly express the grief they felt at his passing.

100 Who tried to steal Lincoln's body?

How's this one for weird? Yes, it's true, someone actually tried to steal Abraham Lincoln's body and hold it for ransom. The story goes like this: In 1876, the engraver from a gang of Springfield, Illinois, counterfeiters went to prison. When the gang's supply of counterfeit scrip began to run low, "Big Jim" Kinealy, who headed up this mob of geniuses, hit upon the idea of breaking into President Abraham Lincoln's Springfield-area crypt, stealing his body, and holding it for ransom in return for the release of the gang's engraver (in addition to $200,000 in gold). Moving the gang's headquarters to Chicago after one of the members got drunk and blabbed about the plot, Big Jim began casting about for coconspirators for the "Lincoln job," and began his search in the saloon he and his gang members frequented. One of the Chicagoans Big Jim befriended and accepted into the gang was in reality an undercover Secret Service agent named Lewis G. Swegles.

Big Jim set the date of the body snatch for election day, November 7, 1876, figuring that there would be fewer people around the Springfield-area cemetery where Lincoln and other members of his family were buried, because they would be busy at the polls.

On Election Day, the gang got through the gate (they sawed the lock off), broke into Lincoln's crypt, and had his coffin halfway out of its place before Swegles gave the signal for police officers lying in wait to spring the trap. (Swegles had been sent out of the crypt to get the horses that would be needed to finish making off with Lincoln's coffin, and that was the moment when he gave the signal for his colleagues to close in.)

The trap did not net a single grave robber that first night. The crooks had been waiting for Swegles and his horses outside the crypt when the police moved in, and they scattered once they realized that they had been caught trying to steal the president's body. Within days the entire gang was apprehended, though, and they all went to trial before a team of prosecuting attorneys Lincoln's eldest son, Robert Todd Lincoln, hired to ensure that they did not get away with the crime. Each gang member (including "Big Jim" Kinealy) got a one-year sentence in Joliet State Prison for his trouble. In part because of this incident, Robert Todd Lincoln eventually had his father's casket removed from the large mausoleum the people of Illinois had erected in his honor, and buried it in a below-ground grave site. And thus ends the tale. Almost reads like the transcript of an episode of *Cops*, doesn't it?

101 The long-term legacy of Abraham Lincoln

The American Communist Party claims Abraham Lincoln as one of its icons, and for years hosted annual Lincoln-Lenin parties in his honor. That statement in and of itself is illustrative of the depth and breadth of the appeal of our sixteenth president, and of the lasting appeal of the cult of Abraham Lincoln. And make no mistake about it: it is a cult. What's more, it's the only cult officially sanctioned by the United States government. In America, Abraham Lincoln is nothing short of a secular saint. Don't think so? Take a look at the Lincoln Memorial. Lincoln sits on a marble throne, looking like nothing so much as a nineteenth-century incarnation of a Greco-Roman god peering out over his assembled worshipers.

Americans have been so loath to relinquish Lincoln to death, that he has been "sighted" multiple times since his murder, in several rooms in various parts of the White House. Legend has it that he appears when the nation is in peril, stomping up and down the halls of the executive mansion, banging on its doors. One of President Benjamin Harrison's bodyguards reportedly attended a séance in hopes of prevailing upon Lincoln's ghost to let him get some sleep. President Calvin Coolidge's wife, First Lady Grace Coolidge, told anyone who would listen that she had once seen Lincoln's ghost in the Oval Office, staring out at the Potomac River.

The sad thing about all of this is that Lincoln the man (like Washington and Jefferson before him) suffers from this marble-statue and ghost-buster treatment. Does Lincoln deserve all of the acclaim he has posthumously received over the past century-plus? Certainly. The problem is, the St. Abraham the American public so reveres bears little resemblance to Lincoln the man.

Oh sure, there are similarities. "Honest Abe" really was honest, scrupulously so. He was also compassionate and absolutely devoted to doing his best to enhance the daily lives of Americans where he thought it both prudent and practicable to do so. By the same token, he was a lifelong pessimist, and frequently had a short memory when it came to personal friendships. An unquestioned political genius who understood how to use his considerable personal charm to get what he wanted, Lincoln is more remembered for the "aw-shucks" folksy character he projected than for the difficult questions he faced throughout his life, how he grew as a human being while president, what he envisioned for his people, or the number of times he failed in his endeavors. We remember that he freed the slaves, when in reality the Emancipation Proclamation did not immediately free anyone. We remember that he was an abolitionist, when he really wasn't, regardless of his personal feelings on slavery. We remember that he had a deep and abiding faith in the people, rather than that he was deeply suspicious of the mob, and of people who could manipulate it. Sometimes we lose sight of the man because we're focused on the more charitable myth. This is one of the lessons history has to teach us.

In the end, who can claim him? Edwin M. Stanton said it best, standing there at the foot of Lincoln's deathbed in April 1865: Abraham Lincoln "belongs to the ages."

Works Consulted

Basler, Roy P., et al., eds. *The Collected Works of Abraham Lincoln.* New Brunswick: Rutgers University Press, 1953.

Dennett, Tyler, ed. *Lincoln and the Civil War in the Diaries and Letters of John Hay.* Cambridge: DaCapo Press, 1988.

Donald, David Herbert. *Lincoln.* New York: Simon & Schuster, 1995.

Donald, David Herbert. *Lincoln Reconsidered: Essays on the Civil War Era.* Reissue ed. New York: Vintage Books, 1989.

Foote, Shelby. *The Civil War: A Narrative History.* 3 vols. New York: Vintage Books, 1986.

Goff, John S. *Robert Todd Lincoln: A Man in His Own Right.* Norman: University of Oklahoma Press, 1968.

Hertz, Emanuel, ed. *The Hidden Lincoln: From the Letters and Papers of William H. Herndon.* New York: Viking Press, 1938.

Holzer, Harold, ed. *Dear Mr. Lincoln: Letters to the President.* Reading, MA: Addison-Wesley Publishing Co., 1993.

McPherson, James M. *Ordeal by Fire: The Civil War and Reconstruction*. New York: McGraw-Hill, 1992.

Mearns, David C., ed. *The Lincoln Papers*. Garden City: Doubleday & Co., 1948.

Miller, William Lee. *Lincoln's Virtues: An Ethical Biography*. New York: Alfred A. Knopf, 2002.

Nevins, Allan. *The War for the Union: War Becomes Revolution*. New York: Charles Scribner's Sons, 1960.

Sandburg, Carl. *Abraham Lincoln*. 3 vols. New York: Dell Publishing Co., Inc., 1954.

Thomas, Benjamin. *Abraham Lincoln*. New York: Alfred A. Knopf, Inc., 1952.

Wellman, Paul I. *The House Divides: The Age of Jackson and Lincoln, from the War of 1812 to the Civil War*. Garden City: Doubleday & Company, 1966.

Wills, Garry. *Lincoln at Gettysburg: The Words That Remade America*. New York: Simon & Schuster, 1992.

Index